D0229213

A Garden in the Hills

A Garden in
the Hills

F
FRANCES LINCOLN LIMITED
PUBLISHERS

ALAN TAIT

For Ciannait

Frances Lincoln Ltd
4 Torriano Mews
Torriano Avenue
London NW5 2RZ
www.franceslincoln.com

A Garden in the Hills
Copyright © Frances Lincoln 2008
Text copyright © Alan Tait
Photographs copyright © Alan Tait
First Frances Lincoln edition: 2008

Alan Tait has asserted his right to be identified as the author of this work in accordance with the Copyright, Designs and Patents Act 1988 (UK).

All rights reserved. No part of this publication may be reproduced, stored in a retrieval system or transmitted in any form, or by any means, electronic, mechanical, photocopying, recording or otherwise, without either permission in writing from the publisher or a licence permitting restricted copying. In the United Kingdom such licences are issued by the Copyright Licensing Agency, Saffron House, 6–10 Kirby Street, London EC1N 8TS.

A catalogue record for this book is available from the British Library.

ISBN 978-0-7112-2926-6

Printed and bound in Hong Kong

9 8 7 6 5 4 3 2 1

Contents

Acknowledgements

At the outset, it may give some encouragement to state the obvious: I have not studied horticulture nor have I worked in any elite garden, public or private, nor am I a botanist. For these reasons, I cannot provide any roll call of the great or skilled that has guided my steps or influenced my thinking. I suppose I am an autodidact of some sort, though this may suggest a rather unpleasant intellectual arrogance. That said, I have listened to gardeners of all kinds and taken note of what they had to say and particularly to Eric Robson, of the National Trust for Scotland, and Sir George Taylor, of Kew, now both gardening in higher altitudes. I have had too and over several decades a landscape rival in Charlie Grimes who, in Pennsylvania, always outdid me in confidence and scale, though he too has crossed the Styx, or rather, as he put it, the Delaware. More immediate and timely in their help were John Saumarez Smith and Murray Grigor. I am quite sure that there are many others to whom I could have listened to more attentively than I did and who would have the satisfaction of hearing their voices, perhaps in laughter, carrying across these pages.

Twenty-four of the photographs were taken for this book by John Reiach, who worked high and low, in and out of rain and always with good humour, to capture the spirit of the place. The remainder are by me. One, however, is reproduced by the kind permission of Mrs. Derek Radcliffe. I am similarly grateful to Anthony Holt for copies of the Gibson letters in his possession and for permission to quote from them here. Lastly, I thank my publisher John Nicoll – adept at skillfully shepherding difficult sheep through his gate.

A. A. T

Preface

All gardens are part of a town or country landscape, always, too, on the move, some faster and more radically than others. Many have come adrift from their setting and are stranded in a no man's land without purpose or meaning and, more disastrously, without identity – the lost garden syndrome of the romantics. The essential balance between house, garden and setting is obviously a subtle one, far easier to destroy than to keep, often difficult to later understand intelligently and certainly to replicate. The task to hold and continue is a hard but not an impossible one, and so it seems to me a worthy theme for a book even if the view taken is a particular if not peculiar one.

I bought the house, and the farm land around it, in various stages between 1972 and 1987. It was an instance of luck where money and opportunity came together at more or less the same time. It had been an upland sheep farm since its final formation in the middle of the eighteenth century, originally of around 6,000 acres, with a farm house and outbuildings of the same time. It was a modest and frugal enterprise, run on a shoestring, a tenant farm on the margins of a large estate, now in trouble. Such comparative poverty helps to explain why so much had survived unimproved, apart from some modernization in the later nineteenth century, best seen in the garden and house. In 1972, it was derelict where sheep, in the logic of *Animal Farm,* had taken over, straying from the fields into the garden and occupying the empty house.

To say I had a clear idea of what I wanted to do from the start would be untrue. But it might be said that I had a latent ambition to be an improver. I had just finished a book on the questionable role of such a figure in the later eighteenth century and I was eager to feel what is was like and understand the passion that drove the improver on to turn marsh into meadow and waste into wood, flinging both caution and money to the wind and achieving as much garden as farm, in the style of the eighteenth century ferme ornée where improvement for pleasure and profit went hand in hand. I wished rather naively to see the past marching into the present and so, I suppose, by including myself, an instance of intellectual vanity. I had too a rich choice of Scottish role models that ran from the agricultural-philosopher Lord Kames at his patrimony to Osgood Mackenzie at Inverewe and Ian Hamilton Finlay at Little Sparta or Sir Henry Steuart and his dancing trees at Allanton in Lanarkshire. On the other hand, there was the rather depressing fact that professionals rarely strayed beyond the page or outside their patron's wishes. Repton and Brown, who created vast landscaped parks at the end of the eighteenth century, never made such a mistake. More recent garden designers, like Lanning Roper or Russell Page, have avoided practical commitment, so much so that the latter's only garden was the tongue in cheek account found in the concluding pages of his *Education of a Gardener*. They rarely practiced what they preached: the garden of the mind was a much easier one to weed.

The circle of the house and its plantations beneath the hill of Carrifran Gans.

For such reasons, it seems sensible enough to deal with landscape as the first and perhaps critical chapter. Any garden, even in a city, is never free of its setting and the more distant and more rural the landscape, the more essential and the more inescapable it becomes. In this instance, it was a strange one. If one looked down from the flight path of the London Scottish flights, the empty valley bottom of 2 miles between steep hills had at its centre a circle of trees and walls that contained the house and buildings and little else, rather like a settler's bivouac prepared for the Indian charge. It had changed little since the planting of the Victorian shelter belts of Scots pine and not much more since the sycamores of the late eighteenth century.

The garden itself presented both problem and solution. It lay to the back of the house and was divided into two by a privet hedge with paths up and down edged by box, all enthusiastically tended by sheep. There were climbing roses, white and red, lots of wild raspberries, rhubarb and abundant nettles. It was easy to put in order and maintain but desperately dull. The solution was to match or balance it on the other side, beside the track leading to the house, with its stylistic opposite, a wild rather than formal garden. It was possible as

The gate, installed in l973, with, beyond it, the start of the beech hedge on a track leading downhill to the house.

Looking from the road down through a rushy field to a grey and derelict house, on offer in l972.

The gate, planting and beech hedge in early autumn, thirty-three years later.

The same view and rushes with a white house thirty-five years on.

well to more or less slip it into the existing landscape. In this fashion, the adjoining plantation of mature Scots pines and decayed dykes or walls provided a home for a small rhododendron garden with, at its edge, the favourite cover of the nineteenth century sportsman, the disparaged but protective *ponticum*.

The buffer was, of course, the house. Once again tact was necessary not to loose its modesty or ignore the odd gesture towards extravagance that ran to the small curved staircase of the original house and its decaying, broad floor boards. The window pattern and the blue-grey colour of the roof slates unconsciously tied it to the stern landscape pattern and brooked little change. Light was always a problem for the abrupt hillsides cut out much that came our way so that the interior had to be sharp, reflective and simple. The rooms, small and dark if left to themselves, needed light in days when the sun arrived after ten and disappeared by three. It shared such problems with the garden. But the house itself was certainly the key and made a pattern that was formal on one side and irregular, perhaps rustic, on the other where the small scale outbuildings of stable and byre formed a long, open courtyard with the dykes and hawthorn hedges.

Great play is often made about consulting the genius of the place. Such an action, it appears to me, is like visiting the classical oracles where riddles rather than answers were given. In my case, the oracle spoke almost by accident. I was standing at the side of the road one day and was asked by a stray motorist if I lived here and would I like to see his old letters about the house. These turned out to be a short series of family letters from 1811 to 1826. They made rather depressing reading for their farming enterprise failed despite their energy and determination. But it was a lesson of encouragement, for I was not the first improver on the ground and might achieve the success that had eluded them. I felt too that the house, garden and farm landscape were waiting patiently with fingers crossed to see who and what might come next.

All authors consider the usefulness or relevance of what they write. As a rule, gardening books are pretty self-explanatory for they belong either to the broadly practical or the descriptive, and sometimes both. Apart from the vain category of behold my works sort, their author's aim is to persuade and encourage; they are seeking converts though they may be read by the converted needing the assurance that they have the right religion. This is my purpose too. I do not think that I have offered any insights into garden or landscape making at all, but I have tried to show that the old tradition of the landscape garden is not dead and can be practiced on a small scale with a reasonable division of time and money – more than can be said for the Pooterish Versailles. As is evident, much has been done on a shoestring, four trees planted instead of six, recycled tree guards and stakes used, grass verges kept less than straight, the scale of the borders often wrong, equipment limited and old-fashioned and so on. I have too brought the house into the landscape equation as more important than just four walls for supporting creepers or squaring a view. In short, this is neither a garden for the public eye in the accepted sense nor the landscape one to catch the breath. There is no insistent injunction to 'Tarry awhile/ amidst flowage'. Instead, it is the strange, promised land of improvement, where so much exists in the mind and the future. And over all hangs a Presbyterian sense that work is good for you – a moral attitude that so fascinated the eighteenth century, Scottish philosophers – and that you may emerge from such an endeavour a better person if not better gardener. Of course, it is much easier to judge the gardener of the two.

I have been vague, perhaps coy, about location for several, modest reasons but it should not be too hard for the determined of purpose to work it all out and much can be seen anyhow from the road. In this way, I have followed the path of Ronald Blythe's *Akenfield* . There are, in the manner of the mystery author, hints enough and no deliberate red herrings, though the solution may disappoint. I have changed or disguised names as well but otherwise I have been honest and helpful. I have not sheltered, for instance, behind some esoteric, garden nickname like 'Ginger', as in a recent American book called *Gardening at Ginger*. My hesitation in all of this has been rather an unwillingness to disappoint or discourage or mislead and so give a new and downward meaning to improvement and the improver's lot.

A.A.T.

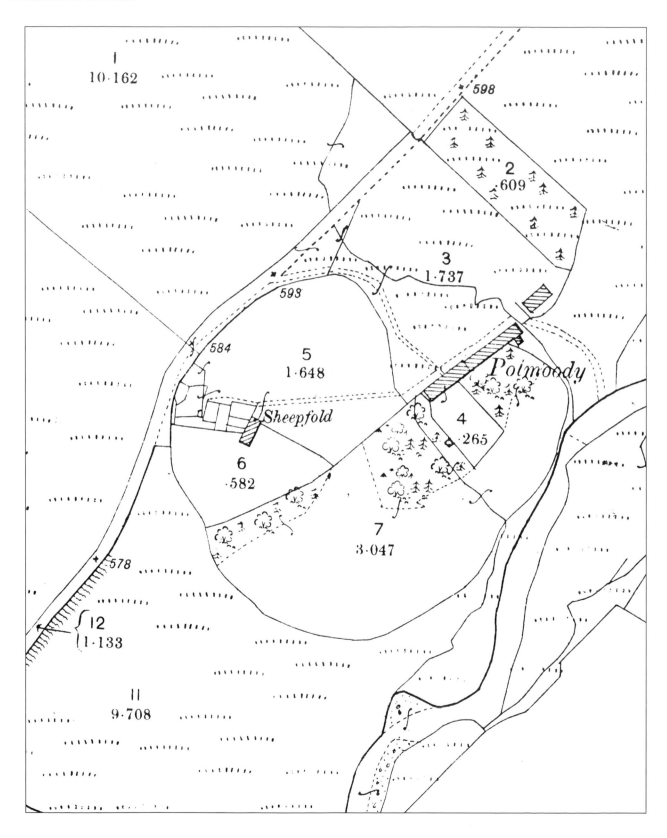

LEFT From the Ordnance Survey
map of 1899.

BELOW Plan of the garden in 2008.

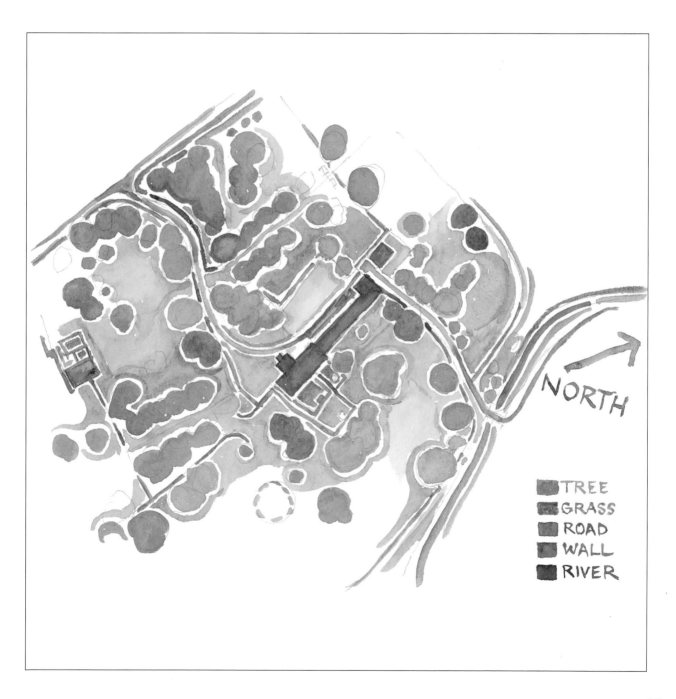

TREE
GRASS
ROAD
WALL
RIVER

NORTH

Introduction

At the entrance looking north into
the valley with Carrifran cottage and
traditional dyke beside the road.

Some time ago, I bought Geoffrey Dutton's *Harvesting The Edge*, which was a saintly tale of gardening on 9 acres in south east Perthshire, the Bridge of Cally in fact, at around 800 feet. The book followed the pattern of the four seasons and unfolded a story of gardening derring-do where the calamities of a winter started in mid-November and where quite severe frosts finished only in mid-June. It was at the end of this tale of horticultural suffering, 'some personal explanations from a marginal gardener' as the byline put it, where the author listed his plants in defensive lines did I realize I was marginal in his sense and, worse, that some of my plant successes were ones from his first and expendable front line. It was a sobering experience and not a particularly uplifting one.

My marginal geography was this. The farm sat at the bottom of a steep and narrow valley where the ground rose quite abruptly from 400 to over 1,000 feet with the hills on both sides offering a gradient of 45 degrees. It was closed at the top eastern end by a hanging valley of some geological importance that also offered a spectacular waterfall with the prosaic title of the Grey Mare's Tail. The other, western end, was more open and allowed, indeed encouraged, a prevailing wind from the south west that swept up and over the house to bounce back again in the opposite direction. Our first postman ruefully remembered riding his bike up the valley against the wind only to have it in his face on the way back. The entry and exit to the valley were marked by two cottages, those of the out-bye shepherds, Carrifran to the west and Birkhill to the east, rather like the tollhouses on the old roads. The reaching of the western point, Carrifran, was signaled by a sheep grid across the crown of the road whose steel bars announced every passerby with a rattle that the hills slavishly repeated. It was the handiwork of the doyen of the local road system who in the early seventies, and in puckish fashion, put up alongside a small gate a sign which read 'Horse drawn vehicles and animals use gate'. It remains and is widely admired as an instance of my playful humour.

The purpose of the grid explained and horse drawn vehicles diverted to one side.

The sheep or cattle grid across the main road with the valley unfolding downhill.

The soil at the bottom of the valley is not rich and in parts is only a few acid inches above the shale, though in the bottom fields it was deeper and richer as well as being a frost pocket. The hillside facing the south east has deep soil and, now that the bracken has been more or less controlled, produces in spring a growing crop of bluebells with the Scottish harebells coming later in the year. It gets the best of sun and light. The valley bottom, and the garden, is on the other hand starved of light and heat during the long winter months. Neither is ever warmed for long and the sun when it appears is shy, making it, diffidently, over the encompassing hills around ten and gone by three. I do have the rather terrifying statistics to support all this and more – best left to the side as unhelpful. Gardening here was, as a former director of Kew, Sir George Taylor, put it, in his distinctly succinct style, an act of faith. Just as well that I was an optimist rather than botanist.

A book such as *Harvesting The Edge* had its limitations for my circumstances. The garden there was essentially an inward looking affair, hidden behind and cut out of the landscape by its sheltering boundaries: very much the oasis syndrome. The type can be found in Finlay's garden at Little Sparta where a few acres are separated from the surrounding, sweeping Lanarkshire moorland though there the spirit was classical, with nature kept at bay rather than on the long rein of Dutton's romanticism. The same laager spirit can be found at Arduaine in western Argyll, where the sea is the aggressor, or in Roy Strong's Laskett, where Herefordshire is rigorously kept at bay. All such exclusive gardens have their souls in the medieval hortus conclusus and turn their backs deliberately on the encircling landscape, like monks in an abbey. I had no wish for such piety nor the need either to hide or retreat from the world and was keen on the rough and tumble of the natural world. But what I did have in common with such gardeners was the less loveable characteristic of control. In none of these cases does the professional garden designer appear either as author or translator and the contract gardener is unwanted: one pair of hands both directs and fulfills. There is, of course, an element of economy in much of this, professional help or advice never comes cheap, as well as a sort of Arts and Crafts integrity, but overall there is a culpable reluctance to delegate or be anything less than master of one's fate.

Looking towards the northern end of the valley from the plantation of 1990 with the house in the middle distance.

Many garden accounts seem to me to be rather lopsided affairs for they fail to give any idea of the expense involved, considerable when a gardener is employed. This is the weakness of the millionaire style of a garden like Les Quatre Vents, on the St.Lawrence in Canada, where costs and labour are explained by having as the next door tenants a landscape contracting business and garden center. There are of course the rather tedious and arch tales of the treasured gardener, inevitably a cantankerous local with a heart of gold, best seen in the snobbish gardening books of Beverley Nichols, of the forties and fifties, and well met in the character of Oldfield in his *Merry Hall*, of 1951. Such books hardly take you far, for hours and pay are never discussed though, for instance, he is inevitably present when the author trips along the terrace to smell the lilies before dinner at eight. A more recent version of this, though altogether kinder and more intellectual, is Peter Smithers *Adventures of a Gardener*, who in his twelve principles included, as two, the unobtainable ideal that the garden 'must therefore be designed and planted so as to reduce labour to a minimum and the work involved must diminish as the owner grows old'. Even the marginal gardener is coy when it comes to money and the considerable costs of deer fencing and setting up a plant nursery are left to one side. Behind such modesty, there is a vague Puritanism that feels such expense is somehow morally wrong and also a smug satisfaction that the less money spent the greater the horticulture skill. Money too is critical in the understanding of what can be achieved: Adam Smith claimed that grapes could be grown in northern Scotland if you were willing to spend enough money on it and this can be seen in the vegetable growing enterprise at present in Achiltibuie in the Summer Isles. The real drain in gardening on any scale is maintenance, the need for time and money to be spent on only standing still which can wear away enthusiasm and drastically curb the imagination. The property pages of any magazine are a fair proof of this.

Need it be said, that when there is a discussion of money there is never complete honesty. To dissemble in some way or another, for some reason or another, is almost natural, as is the operation of some sort of code that can be read between the lines. Few people will admit to buying a white elephant – at least not until it has been sold – and many confuse investment with indulgence. It was into the latter that I can fairly put myself, for I saw my acquisition as an experiment, satisfying both physically and intellectually, though I also persuaded myself, against reason, that it was money well spent. It needed comparatively little capital but a great deal of income and became like some fat cuckoo in the domestic nest, turfing out the nestlings of renovation and decoration as well as prescribing summer holidays. In l972, when the house and roughly 5 acres of land were bought from the Forestry Commission, the going rate for a gardener was about £6,000 to which had to be added all the paraphernalia of the welfare state. Should I have wanted such a person it was not feasible financially. As it was, the annual £500 spent on plants and trees were as much as could be afforded. In this light, I was not particularly impressed to read in Jane Taylor's *Weather in the Garden*, that to consider a plant too tender it was necessary to 'have personally killed it three times' – an expensive pastime.

Hand in hand with the matter of money went that of time. This was always in comparatively short supply for I was a city dweller with a job and children, though I did have fairly generous vacations – at least at first. Gardening was generally limited to weekends and this often proved an advantage, for it provided the week for rumination or meditation on what had been done and what was on the cards. I took heart from the account of the lawyer Lord Kames who, on his return to the country from court in Edinburgh, went out in the dark immediately to look at his plantations by lantern light. Such a routine worked well for my small plantations and specimen trees, but it did severely limit what could be achieved in the garden proper. Any form of flower garden was really out of the question, for day to day maintenance, such as weeding, planting out and staking could not be done. And this applied also to any type of vegetable growing that needed regular labour. However, I did relent in making hedges. I have always seen them as the bones of any garden and indeed landscape, especially when there is a long winter period and where they appear as an essay in minimalism, one just as easy to get wrong as right. I inherited a small one of green privet and planted further ones of yew, beech and hawthorn, some needing more attention than others, but all kept around 6 feet. All of this, of course, concentrated the mind, albeit in a somewhat negative fashion.

A further aspect of the time equation was scale. The house came with 5 acres that I quickly increased to 15, of which half an acre was garden in the broadest sense. Later, I acquired the adjoining forest and then the remains of the old farmland that brought the whole to a bit over four thousand. The garden was then expanded to almost 2 acres. As part of this escalation, the enclosed field beside the house was taken in and given a park-like treatment with trees thickened at the boundary walls and single trees planted in a random pattern to suggest extent, in a manner perhaps more Brown than Repton. Ironically, all of this was matched by a sharp decline in the amount of free time I had, though I still resisted, fiercely, regular help on any scale. The argument for such foolish independence was that my plans were always in my head and not on paper and so could never be entrusted to even the most sympathetic helper. This was compounded by a healthy suspicion of machinery and gadgets. However, I did have a rather expensive motor mower where the grass cuttings had to be raked up afterwards, though this doubled as moss control, as well as hand shearers for the hedges and tree-pruners, forks, spades, edgers and others of a Luddite sort. I still use a stainless steel spade I bought in l972, and my favourite pair of shears came from my parent's garden and represented over fifty years of toil. On the short driveway, in the yard and on the paths I used weedkiller. And that was that. Three continuous days of work are needed to bring a reasonable standard of control and order.

The landscape was looked after in a similar fashion though here I had less control. Fencing and gates were done by contractors, as was the banking of the wandering Moffat Water, and they replaced as well two footbridges. Some alleged commercial planting was also undertaken. However, the repair and renewal of the dykes was my concern and the several miles of these battered, but unbowed, bastions offered plenty of opportunity. In the two fields surrounding the house and garden, I imported a flock of Soay sheep, displaced persons from the island of that name, which needed little attention – they molted rather than were sheared – and they kept the grass under control but had a sweet tooth for a new tree. For more serious matters, such as dosing for the tick mite, they were dealt along with the commercial blackface sheep, of which there were about 1,200 breeding ewes on the farm. But with these sheep, I was out of step with the improver. My predecessors had all tried cross breeding to improve either the wool or the body weight, whereas I retrogressed into introducing the pre-Roman sheep that gave poor wool and less meat though they had a great advantage of robust self-sufficiency. They also looked good as well as being a walking history lesson in evolution and so appealed to me, academically and aesthetically. For I snobbishly had in mind the early nineteenth century prints from Neale's *Views of Seats in Scotland*, where deer and sheep stared dotingly at their owners' house in the middle distance across the parkland.

If there is only one joke in the world then all gardens are descended from that in Eden. However, there is a long way between this one and any form of Eden and the path between the two is particularly tortuous. In plotting such as descent, I have tried to avoid the genealogist's trap, where the great and famous of cultural history are claimed as forbears, both visually and imaginatively, or, where through some deep process of osmosis, a union of sorts is sealed.

Looking down the hill from the new plantation to the river running downstream to the southern march dykes.

Apart from family gardens, none of which were in any way remarkable, the formative force was the enjoyable decade I spent on the garden committee of the National Trust for Scotland. From such a heady perch, I not only judged a considerable range of historic and not so historic gardens from Arduanie to Hill of Tarvit, but also several that the Trust for one reason or another had not taken on. The committee trips were remarkable: two day affairs where about eight of us swooped down in a convoy of cars, led and disciplined by the garden advisor, on some hapless, national treasure and its nervous guardians. It was a scene that would have fed the dullest of imaginations but offered alongside a supremely critical standard in action, fastidiously separating the outstanding from the very good and on down the scale. Such gardens showed what might be achieved in a lifetime or half a lifetime, what neglect could manage in five years and what one pair of hands should take on. At the end of such visits, we probably all returned home to kick or pat the garden.

Such was my immediate, visual education that went hand in hand with reading. In looking along my bookshelves, it is tempting to identify, presumptuously, with the great gardening heroes like William Robinson or Gertrude Jekyll and pass over the powerful influence exerted by the more run of the mill authors. If a single source can be plucked from such a generality, it was probably something as basic as Hilliers' *Manual of Trees and Shrubs*, of which I have still my faded hardback copy of 1972. I can explain such a choice. Before I started gardening, I was interested in plant identification and later on found the various indexes at the end that grouped trees and shrubs by the flowering month as well as by category. By this means, I was furnished with a list of plants for particular situations with that for 'cold, exposed areas' especially interesting to me after 1972. The then unillustrated *Manual* had invented, or so it seemed, a wonderful code that gave a tactful but clear assessment of the merits of any tree or shrub. 'Useful' really meant for a blind botanist only, 'charming' was certainly loaded, 'valuable' hardly praise, while 'elegant' and 'striking' were definitely terms of approval though meaning different things in different situations. It was a practical and clinical approach to gardening, eminently objective, and just the thing for the aspiring improver with its nice blend of enthusiasm, knowledge, caution and lack of flowery, catalogue language. It was realistic. Though the list for the cold and exposed made rather gloomy reading and cast those from Dutton's marginal gardening as almost exotic in comparison, it gave sensible confidence. Encouragingly, the *Manual* seemed to suggest that there were worse places to garden, much colder, wetter and even more exposed, and that I was not quite on the horticultural rim, just nearly so.

Balancing the influence of the *Manual* was my source for landscape inspiration, the *Oxford Book of Trees*, a well illustrated, in the diagrammatic sense, account of the evolution of the arboreal countryside. I probably acquired it around the same time as I did several distinctly less useful books. Perhaps the most interesting aspect of the book was its determination to see trees and undergrowth as one and a mixed landscape of conifers and deciduous as natural, making a particularly strong case for the yew (*Taxus baccata*) and so for the non-native podocarpus and juniper. Such an interest in the native encouraged a curiosity about the elm of which there were some outstanding examples here of its Scotch form (*Ulmus glabra*), planted in the nineteenth century. This led to my rashly planting its various forms, especially the golden elm (*Ulmus glabra* 'Lutescens') fatally of course, for they all were gradually killed by elm disease, death depending on how close they were to the river and its deadly flotilla of leaves. In retrospect, this catastrophe underlined the Oxford lesson that nature never relied heavily on one species in one spot, a lesson that the Forestry Commission has yet to learn.

The Forestry Commission, or Forest Authority, was until the sales of the l990s my most immediate and large neighbour, casting a dark and baleful shadow over the valley, and destroying its social structure. It had bought up three of the nearby farms, and most of this one as well, and then planted the 12,000 acres with Norway and Sitka spruce in strict geometrical fashion. There was little of the concept of improvement here or of any aesthetic concerns even in the broadest sense: their remit was to plant cheap trees and they stuck to it regardless. The commission, set up in l919, had changed its skin several times and was now locked into the State Forest idea, one distantly and old-fashionably related to both the American New Deal and Russian social realism of the l930s. So much so, that it was sincerely claimed by one of its admirers in l962 that 'wherever there are State forests one may be sure of finding a friendly welcome'. In such a spirit, it had created in seigneurial fashion the forest village of Ae in Dumfriesshire, some twenty miles away, where identical houses were grouped around a village green in the heart of a vast wood in a setting worthy of the brothers Grimm. In this valley, the result of such casual social and physical engineering, was a checker board of decaying farms and rising forests with the natural contours gone and

The old and new, a march dyke
with a fence to the forestry
plantation of Sitka spruce and
autumn bracken.

the old system of dykes and fields all but obliterated. This whole sorry story was well aired from the naturalist's point of view in the *Galloway and the Borders* volume of the New Naturalists Library, ironically partly written from this house.

A more modern, aesthetic improver might see things differently. It could be argued, though the Forestry Commission never has, that its vast forests cast in a perpetual and uniform mid-green and stamped in an arbitrary fashion over the existing pattern were a form of land art. For, in absolute terms, there is not much to distinguish its methods and their effect from the land forms shaped into James Turrell's Roden Crater in Arizona or the grid-like lines of steel poles in Walter De Maria's Lightning Fields. It was not a route I was tempted to follow. I wished instead a visual compromise, a balance between the old and new landscapes, and one sympathetic to what they were about, for not every tree was bad or sheep good and the lion could lie down with the lamb. The eye was, of course, the absolute judge in all this but it was also dangerously selective, conservative and not always truthful. It registered, as often as not, what was in the mind rather than on the ground and its henchman in such enterprises was the photographer. The part the photographer could play was ideally described by Edwin Smith in his *All the Photo-Tricks,* where he saw the camera as 'one step further from the tyranny of everyday appearance, and one nearer the world of ideas, granting power to suppress prosaic fact in favour of creative imagination'.

In a great many books about gardens and landscapes illustrations are chosen on their own terms – rightly so for a poor or dull photograph is just that – but they often lose all sense of place, what in wine circles is known as *terroir.* No matter how attractive the large, close-to shot of the 'Bobbie James' rose, it could be from anybody's garden and tells more about the plant, its health, possibly its owner, and certainly the photographer's skills than anything else. Such words may be seen as a less than subtle form of apologia for a run of difficult images that perhaps reveal a better sense of history than beauty. I hope not; for in documenting improvement there has to be a strong element of the before and after, perhaps not quite like Repton's tantalizing system of flaps, but along similar lines. Something of this may be grasped from the rather artless plan that I have included more for identification than rigorous, critical analysis. It is coded by colour – blue for river, green for grass – and so makes clear the essential elements of the landscape and the pattern they make together. I have also used photographs in a similar fashion to document the trinity of the landscape, garden and house, all with a strong *terroir* bent. I have wanted to show, too, the various layers of a scene in a state of flux as well as the enduring elements of the place that perhaps shrug off change as at best facile and superficial. It is case of setting the record straight. It is clear too from the pictures that I hold photography as one of several ways of recording and interpreting, neither better nor worse than say drawing, only a different means to an end. With that said, a book such as George Courtauld's *An axe, A spade and Ten Acres,* of 1983, which had pen drawings in the text but no photographs, seemed to lack any visual thrills and leave the text stranded and forlorn. In looking over my thrills, I have been struck by the seeming exclusion of people, or animals, to animate and enliven any scene. They have been there, of course, for their footprints show in the width of a path, or gate, or a garden bench and the whole landscape reverberates to human endeavour, the endless and satisfying struggle with nature. The chapters that follow should be the proof of this.

Landscape

The river curving towards the house
with the long line of the dykes of the
lambing fields to one side.

At the outset, I claimed to be an improver in the eighteenth century sense, that is to say where improvement led not only to changes in the landscape but to the betterment of the people who lived there and in so doing improved the improver. It was a reworking of the simple moral that virtue was its own reward. With this in mind, I am far from sure that my predecessors fall into such a category. Improvers they certainly were but they were almost exclusively concerned with animals and husbandry, as they had a living to earn and little time or money for much else. They were also tenant farmers on a large estate and so their hands were tightly tied and they passed through the valley unremarkably and anonymously. There was an exception, the Gibson family of the early nineteenth century, whose surviving letters from the house suggest that such silent witnesses were often both thoughtful and determined and remarkably adventurous .

Thomas Gibson and his family came from Traquair in western Peeblesshire where they had been tenants at Westerglen. This was a move from one upland sheep farm to another in a similar country. The first surviving letter of the batch was written from Edinburgh in 1811 by Gibson's son John, one of four, to his sister Isabella, one of three. It was thoroughly domestic, mainly about health – there was a nurse Nell Brydon in the house – and domestic affairs. His sister Helen was still 'carrying on with her pet lamb', the youngest brother Alexander, away at school at Yarrow and he riding down on a pony with the family to church, presumably in Moffat. It also offered a glimpse of the typical farm garden that existed then: 'you may let me know how the garden is coming on and if there is likely to be any berries this year'. The berries were probably blackcurrants and gooseberries and the question suggests the uphill struggle of growing things successfully even in the low-walled garden. A letter of 1816, to Francis Gibson from the house, recounts a trip made by Isabella and a neighbour Mary Beck to go sea bathing on the Solway estuary at Kirkbean, where 'most part of the road which I went is exceedingly wild. The farm houses are very bad, few of them exceed one storey and they are all thatched'. This suggests that their own house was slated, rather thatched, and of more than one story. The wildness referred to in the letter, too, was about to change decisively for a further letter referred to a company of the Royal Artillery, stationed on top of the encircling Moffat hills, 'measuring the height of the mountains and drawing an exact map of the country'. This was part of an ambitious and detailed survey made to follow on from Kirkwood's more straightforward map of Dumfriesshire, published in 1807, a copy of which hangs in the house.

The Gibsons were an intelligent and progressive family, especially interested in education. One brother, in December 1816, wrote to the other in Edinburgh asking, 'what you are reading in Latin' and 'if you can get a French Dictionary which has the pronunciation'. The basis of their learning was the small school at Yarrow, beside the church and some fifteen miles away on the road to Selkirk, which had a considerable local reputation at this time under the headmastership of John Scott. He had been appointed in 1784 and remained there until 1818 and took in some twenty to thirty boarders whom he charged £8 per session at first and then later between £18 and £20. For this, the pupils – all boys – were taught to read and write and then moved on to English grammar, arithmetic and geography. Later, after 1816-17, French and Latin were added to the syllabus. Bearing in mind the background of his charges, Scott also taught land measurement and the making of paper plans. However, the boys had to make their own arrangements for the provisions that were sent by a weekly carrier along with letters from the house that always asked how 'your clothes and shoes are lasting'. None of this and the support for a son wishing to study law in Edinburgh came without cost and put a strain on the limited resources of a tenant farmer, even an entrepreneurial one.

In 1818, it all came to an end. Gibson gave up his tenancy and took on another farm just over the hill where he stayed only two years until moving to London and success. With the end of the Napoleonic war, farming was starting its long decline and Gibson summarized the situation with candor. He wrote dispassionately that 'by a calculation of considerable length the accuracy of which may be relied upon, I have endeavoured to show (and I think plainly) that the present failure has been occasioned not so much through rashness or bad policy as some may be apt to suppose but through a cause of forseen losses which it was impossible to prevent being lost since the farm was taken'. How this came about is difficult to determine but it does suggest that expenditure was always ahead of income, even in the good years. Though Gibson had the help of his sons and daughters, there was apparently a need for additional labour that was supplied by the Boa family in the cottage and steading at the far end of the valley. They cost Gibson £20 a year in addition to an allowance of potatoes, oatmeal and coal, and the right to graze twenty-one sheep and a cow. The Boas, William and Walter, fared better than the Gibsons and they lasted on the farm until 1887.

It is likely that much of the physical form of the farm took shape during the twenty-two years of the Gibson regime and with the connivance of the estate. Their most obvious contribution was the system of dykes, necessary if there was to be any form of systematic breeding and this would suggest the 1780s. Some of the fields, at the bottom of the valley, were probably formed at this time and they may have been used for taking off a crop of hay for winter feeding of both the sheep and the farm horses. In addition, there were gathering enclosures that held the sheep for clipping and dipping. The present fanks (pens) and the building associated with them were probably rather later, and the various smallish, circular stells positioned up and down the valley, where sheep could be kept overnight and in bad weather, were possibly earlier. The planting with sycamores around the edges of the oval field beside the house was, by their girth, done by Gibson, as was the planting of a small kitchen garden for the berries. Of all these improvements, the formation of the walling pattern over the valley and hillsides was the most obviously visible and one that, by and large, survived fairly well and usefully until the advent of the Forestry Commission.

A system of dykes was a practical affair: the surface stones, cleared from the fields or taken from the rocky outcrops on the hill, composed the building material for both dykes and the house and so achieved a remarkable uniformity. The real difference between the two lay in the use of mortar as a bonding material, in the house and outbuildings, and its absence in the drystane dykes. The lime mortar allowed a wall of any height whereas its lack limited the wall, no matter how cleverly constructed, to below roughly 7 feet. Not that this mattered much, for the black faced sheep – even with the improved breeds – rarely got over a wall of 4 feet and, if properly shepherded, would not so much as try. The alternatives to walls, hedges or fences, did not exist until the last century. Thus, flying over the landscape like some crow, the valley appeared below with a small, twisting river in the centre with, on either side, the rectangles and squares of the fields and their walls like some gigantic grid squeezed between the angles of the hillsides. The dykes also introduced an element of colour; the various enclosures produced

Sheep gathered for the pens with the original sycamores circling the house.

an intense green while the fields without gave a lighter one, and the greens were contrasted with the upper hill slopes of grey of shale and rock and the blues of heather and blaeberries in the summer. Such a basic pattern of colour, shape and size was only disturbed at one part where, on a gentle east facing slope, there were potato furrows, successor to the medieval terracing that existed still further up and under the shade of the conifers.

The walls themselves are almost impossible to date, for the way they were put together was almost unchanging. All that did change was perhaps the skill and sophistication of the builder, who was inevitably a shepherd, for their building and repair were traditionally part of his duties. The type of wall constructed here, and in the western part of the county at least, was a double wall with outer surfaces chipped by hammer to make a smooth dyke up to nearly 3 feet, one that would refuse any marauding sheep a foothold. Between the two walls was an infilling of small stones, heartening is the term. The two walls were then bridged by a flat through stone on to which were piled large, rough boulders, loosely joined with on top rounded capstones. Ideally, the capstones should form a regular surface along which a wheelbarrow could be run easily and smoothly. Behind all of this, there was a subtle blend of the physical and physiological warfare where the simple height and roughness of the wall was balanced, at eye level, by the sudden light and glare through the gaps. It was a bold sheep who could cope with such tactics. In judging the age of these dykes, it is the contrast between the rough and the smooth surfaces that distinguished early from late, as well as the wall height: as a rule of thumb the older the wall, the lower. There is too, the variation known as the Galloway dyke, where a hawthorn hedge was grown from behind and over the lower wall. It never worked here nor does it appear in any of the older farms around. Where a modern wall – that is of the last fifty years – is built, it makes the mistake of continuing the small stones right up until a single course of regular capstones, often laid on the diagonal. The distribution of weight is wrong and the wall basically unstable though it may be decorative and, as often as not, is the handiwork of an artisan – dyker rather than the shepherd.

As with the Forestry Commission, the hand of ministerial officialdom has almost been as destructive. In the seventies, the then Department of Agriculture handed out generous grants for wire fencing but nothing for the repair, or rebuilding, of the dyke system. In fact, in the bright new world of farming, walls were seen as old-fashioned and inefficient, just like old farm buildings whose demolition was also actively encouraged. Stone, no matter how fashioned, was a problem for them. It looked and smelt too much of the past and lacked the feel of industrial systems. I doubt if they understood or sympathized with the Langholm poet, Hugh MacDiarmid and his stoney world, however local, of 'Ratchel, striae, relationship of tesserae/ Innumerable shades of grey/ Innumerable shapes/ And beneath them all a stupendous unity'. The survival of such walls had to do with reverse economics, the poorer the farm, the less money for fences and the like, particularly true in hill farms such as this. And so matters stood when I came along, with ugly and broken down fencing near the house and miles of dykes, often in total disrepair, beyond: all grist to the improver's mill.

The next element in the basic landscape pattern was trees or rather plantations. The forest above the house, part of a larger one, was planted with a dull mixture of Sitka and Norwegian spruce. Amongst them on dryer ground were hybrid larch and some sycamore at the bottom edges, with the residual birch popping up here and there. It was only the larch that charted the change of seasons and introduced variety into the staid green-blue blanket of the spruce. In forestry terms, the timber is poor and would never make a marketable crop of any value and certainly not repay the costs of extraction on such steep land. To join the various large and small plantations in some form of visual harmony, I planted a similar mixture along the valley bottom with deciduous trees and the odd exotic, such as the wellingtonias and *Calocedrus decurrens*, predominating as they surrounded and closed in upon the house. The idea of making some kind of conifer collection, the Victorian pinetum, did not appeal. My range would have been too limited to have any effect. Apart from the Scots pine and odd examples of Bhutan, *cembra*, *banksiana*, *nigra*, none of the other pines did and, anyhow, I much preferred the silver firs that kept their sweeping downward branches and conical form. I had as well, at the back of my mind, the idea of creating the illusion of a fertile valley bottom with a wide range of species that became more limited as they thinned out and climbed the sides of the hills to the bare (or not so bare) tops. In planting over the skyline, the Commission had radically changed the shape of the entire valley and the amount of sunlight it received. Before its arrival in the early sixties, the hills had been quite bare, with a few rowans and birches at the edges of the burns, and the odd, stunted hawthorn on the slopes under the lee of a large rock. In the late spring, all being well, these hawthorns gave a magnificent display of white blossom that seemed almost frivolous in such a stern and wild landscape. It was a mistake about which little could be done in the short term, cutting them out would only make matters worse and change the woods taxable status from commercial to amenity and attract the interest of the taxman.

In all of this, it is clear that I accepted the landscape as found, with emphasis put on the restoration end of improvement. Unlike many of my kind, I was not interested in the visible effect of carving out a new kingdom for myself and was keener to be thought of as subtle and deep, rather than obvious and superficial. This stance ruled out any buildings, or the like, anywhere apart from the garden, as they would set up different values for the landscape into which they were foisted. On the other hand, I have always admired well designed gates, good walls and keen husbandry, much more than a landscape of artificial viewpoints and sculpture silhouetted against the skyline. Moreover, I have practiced, where I can, what I have preached: the gates to the fields around the house are metal, five barred, painted white and a combination of old and new, traditional and serviceable, those to the further fields are wooden of the plain, commercial sort. Such a utilitarian theme has been continued on the main bridge that crosses the river just below the house. The ruined one of the sixties was replaced in 1990 by a simple, wooden structure of old joists on two steel beams, designed by a Border firm of structural engineers. They rest on buttresses on either bank of river stones in a steel mesh, pegged by spikes to the river bottom and protected by large rocks brought down from the hillside. Moss and rushes have now moved in and small rowans planted to one side of the northern ends have taken – slowly. It fitted well with the obvious character of the rutted sheep tract that crossed the river to the dyked, lambing fields on the other side. As a reward, it offered a viewing platform on which to lean and look east and west, up and down the river, as Repton advised in much grander circumstances, while speculating on the lack of fish.

I have occasionally strayed from such a puritanical path but only in a minor sort of way and my major misdemeanor had been the most recent. A short, straight and wet path through the Old Plantation, with an edge of hybrid rhododendrons, *Juniperus communis* and yew, comes

LEFT Looking upstream on a winter's afternoon from the snowy bridge.

RIGHT Looking south along the bulwarks towards the rebuilt bridge.

On the handrail of the oak stile are carved in succinct form the mileage up and down the river.

to sheep fence with the open haughlands of the valley beyond. At this point, there was a small, narrow stile that I have replaced with a more ambitious affair, since removed to the watergate at the river. It has steps, a handrail and is made from old oak and is shamelessly derived from that at Ian Hamilton Finlay's Little Sparta, as illustrated in most of the books about the garden. I have dropped his punning and elliptical inscriptions for the more prosaic distance markers to the towns east and west. Like Finlays's work too, it was made by other hands and, in this case, a country furniture maker living nearby. It makes few demands on its setting beside the wire fence and is only really apparent through the easy passage its offers the less agile walker. Nonetheless, it points in the wrong direction intellectually and shows how easy it would be to be deaf or blind to the simplicity of the place. Temptation is always there, and there was a time when a small faux doocot, serving as a store for dipping equipment, white harled with a slate roof, on the raised mound of an old, flattened stell, visible except for the few months of high summer, beckoned but was shunned. I felt it would insert into the landscape the marker memorial concept and all the emotional baggage that inescapably goes with such monuments. Even the traditional cairn of rough stones piled at the top of some hill seemed to me suspect in this simple, barren and unassuming landscape and its absence all the more evocative. Sculpture beyond the garden was also suspect, for its sophisticated and heavily worked forms demanded a quite artificial response from its setting, if it was not to be ruthlessly overwhelmed by it. I felt this was true of the famous *King and Queen* of Henry Moore, at Glenkiln in Dumfriesshire, ensconced to grandly survey a grouse moor and a not too distant public reservoir, and equally so of Barbara Hepworth's work when installed outside a garden. Such an argument can be found in the sculptor Anthony Caro's essay of 1983, where 'sculpture in my opinion more often than not spoils landscape', and, put the other way around, 'landscape by and large is a greater defeater, particularly majestic or informal landscape'. Such sculpture appeals as the drama of the unexpected but does little over time, when drama fades, to enhance the natural state or the historic vista. The early eighteenth century tradition, where the landscape was treated as a garden, formed as a spacious green gallery, was closer to my way of thinking, as it offered a more sympathetic home for such tactile works of art.

To turn away totally from all sculpture in the landscape or garden is excessively prescriptive: it is an essential element in too many places even if it takes the form of the debased bird-bath. I have settled for sculpture on a minor and decorative key, much of which is topical, rather than timeless, and brash, rather than smooth or sophisticated. My two medieval heads on the wall of the ante-garden, peering through rose leaves at visitors, have nothing to say with their lolling tongues and no statement of any kind to make. In the yard, fixed on the gable wall of the garage is a plastic, vividly coloured, ice cream cone with chocolate stick, a piece of Pop, which if nothing else harks back to the original notice of 'cigarettes sold here'. There are as well two simple notices, one *Visite des Caves*, the other *Azienda Faunistico Venatoria*, one placed at the entrance to the washing machine and drying area and the other on the east fence of the Old Plantation that excludes deer. They are in the distant tradition of the childish, garden joke where water jets surprised the unwary and the common element to them all is faint humour. They continue where the sheep grid notice of 'Horse drawn vehicles' left off.

The key to this landscape is the hills: they dominate by shape, colour and scale, and the stone of which they are composed has rooted the buildings in the ground. They are an essay in geological history too, for the retreating glacier rounded the hill tops and left its rocky debris scattered along the valley bottom. At the northern end, it left a hanging valley with a long waterfall spanning, as it were, the two levels of evolution with the fossil fish, graptolites, at its foot as the imprint of older life. All of this was explored and explained by Charles Lapworth, who used the cottage at Birkhill at the head of the valley, the former home of the Boas, as the research base for his Moffat Series of 1878. The bedrock of much of the valley becomes immediately apparent to any planter when scratching the surface for a pocket of soil for even the most modest of tree. Not content with such absolute power, the hills also regulate the amount of light and sunlight and catch and hold the clouds and mists. They can be your friend or foe but should never be neglected.

The hills express some concept of freedom too, of life without anything but natural restriction, and this spirit was at the heart of the Covenanting history of the valley, in the later seventeenth century. The Covenanters, a strongly left wing and intolerant religious group, sought refuge in the hills in the south west and especially in this valley, where they were hunted by the government troops and ruthlessly shot on

LEFT A modern plastic ice cream cone, of commercial provenance, wall mounted on the garage gable as a piece of Jeff Koons sculpture.

RIGHT An Italian notice at the stile to the Old Plantation, warning the deer that this is an *Azienda Faunistico Venatoria*.

sight. Undeterred, they held their Sunday services hidden in the hills with watchers posted strategically to warn of trouble and so one such hill, to the north of the house, was called Watch Knowe for that reason. Some of this appeared in *The Brownie of Bodesbeck*, the historical novel by James Hogg, the Ettrick Shepherd. Bodesbeck was one of the neighbouring farms and originally the name to our telephone number, outdone in the literary stakes only by Edinburgh Waverley. Much the same feeling for freedom and refuge appears in the adventure story of *The Thirty-Nine Steps* by John Buchan. Written as the horror of the First World War became apparent in 1915, its hero, Richard Hannay, takes to the hills to avoid both police and villains and spends his last night on the Moffat hills before catching the train south at Beattock. For him, they provided both 'the miseries of that night among the wet hills' and the 'shining blue weather with a constantly changing prospect of brown hills and far green meadows', extremes that echoed pretty well the fortunes of Hannay himself.

From what I have written, I seem to have suggested that the setting is all and this may well be close to the truth – equally true of the town as the country garden and the urban or rural setting. There is of course the alternative, to turn your back on the setting altogether and shut it out completely, in the style of the medieval hortus conclusus. Yet, no matter whether the setting is landscape or townscape, it is always a practical

A tin vineyard sign set on the wall beside the door to the boiler house.

affair shaped by either the industrial or agricultural revolution and almost all have a sense of history, or at least of place. In all such settings, the garden ekes out a living at the mercy of economic and physical forces, and depends on the goodwill of fate, a risky business at the best of times. For the marginal garden, such as this, the stakes are higher, the chips more expensive and rules inflexible. It can be grudgingly accepted as part of such a setting, but always on the understanding that little should be taken for granted, beyond perhaps hope, and that it can only be a small player in such an empty and barren landscape of overpowering integrity.

The civilizing or humanizing force in such a stark setting is a sense of history. There can be few landscapes where it is absent or, where the local historian or writer has not created some sense of identity, or the painter captured an ideal from them. D.Y. Cameron, the great visionary of the Scottish hills, particularly the Highland ones, wrote of them that 'out of these shadows of the centuries, veiled by distance or muted by fading light and gathering darkness, there emerged great figures or actions' and his dark painting of Criffel on the Solway, of around 1907, was just that. I saw it from my window every day as a child. In the county next door, that of Selkirk, the limping ghost of Walter Scott stalks the hills and valleys. His presence, here, is even more palpable for he seems to have rattled past the door en route for Moffat in August 1826, possibly while Thomas Carlyle was asleep in an upstairs bedroom, if tradition is to be believed. He took his lunch at Birkhill 'under the moist and misty influence of the Genius Loci', so presumably ate inside. As the great improver of Abbotsford and the unkindly critic of Sir Henry Steuart at Allanton, Scott has always been a presence, encouraging me to feel the spirit of my hills. At Abbotsford, Scott could hear from the distance the talk of the soldiers on Hadrian's Wall, could see the monks of Melrose Abbey and watch the ill-fated Scottish army assembling for Flodden Field, all in the acute memory of the eye. He treasured such a possession more than sight itself and, on his last journey to Abbotsford in 1832, he could point out 'Gala water, Buckholm, Torwoodlee', more feeling than seeing them. Such was the role of landscape.

At the northern end of the valley with pass and cottage at Birkhill where graptolites were discovered and Sir Walter Scott ate his lunch.

The Garden

Looking down from the hill into the
sheep fanks showing the pattern of
dykes and stone shed, all probably of
the mid-nineteenth century.

A small house and small garden must struggle to have any sort of identity in the larger landscape of their setting. Too modest and they disappear into the landscape, overly aggressive and they seem out of place. So to fit in, they must also make some sort of sense of their position, just as the farm and its fields do, or the cottage and the inbye land, or even the country house and its tame parkland. In all of these cases, the sum is greater than the parts and there is no sadder sight than the landless farm or denuded country house. The opposite is true as well; that the land needs a domestic element even if it seems little more than a detail in the great scheme of things. Most journeys through rural Scotland sooner or later encourage such pessimistic thinking. This was so when I first crossed the sheep grid on the public road and went down into the valley with its tiny grey farm and circle of trees plum in the centre, like some oasis or fort awaiting an Indian attack. At this time, 1973, the forestry plantations were in their infancy and so the bracken clad hills rose cleanly and boldly with a sharp profile from 500 feet to 1,200 at their peaks of greywacke. The effect was the identity crisis of my first sentence, for the almost savage power of the setting made the house seem both fragile and resolute, and its garden appear as some exotic luxury.

Colour plays its part in all of this, though grey and green, and their tones, are the extent of the limited range. Grey is the colour of the rocky outcrops and of the river during the long winter months and is repeated in the snaking lines of the dykes with a blue tone in the slate roofs of farm buildings. The new hillside plantations of Norway and Sitka spruce are of an unchanging and relentless blue-green, broken only in wintertime by the brown of the hybrid larch and the decayed bracken at their feet. In too many cases, these trees disappear over and hide the skyline, with the result that the landscape seems darker and more uniform, and it was only with the belated arrival of the landscaper Sylvia Crow in 1977 that they were given irregular boundaries and dropped below the hilltops. There is also beyond the

Larch was planted on the east and western slopes of the valley in the early seventies and can give a downward view through bracken such as this one.

Low water on the autumn river with the larch and grass on the hillside brown.

house and just to the east what remains of a nineteenth century shelter belt, now the Old Plantation as though in Louisiana, planted to protect the sheep in the gathering field from the forceful north east wind. As in many hill farms, this forlorn belt of blasted Scots pines and its enclosing dyke were in disrepair, housing rather than sheltering the sheep, and the gaunt, surviving pines seemed to reproach the vitality and youth of the surrounding conical spruce. It was to bring the two together that I planted two further rectangular plantations in the shelter belt style, one along the roadside to the east, the other west of the house, in 1986 and 89. While this may have spoilt the cowboys and indians effect, it made the best of the cards dealt and introduced, in volume, trees that were not conifers. The larger, and more successful western one, was predominantly beech that grew well on the south facing slope to the river: the eastern one of birch, alder and sycamore has done badly on boggy ground and has been replanted twice. Sad to say, both are fenced, because improvements grants were then only for fencing, and so they lack the rough character of their older neighbour.

Alongside all three of the shelter belts ran the public road, narrow, ferociously twisted and generously served by both potholes and poor ditches. It followed the course of a traditional tract that ran eastwards beside the river to Selkirk and was a traditional, popular excursion route in the later nineteenth century. It had some claim to fame as well, as the path followed by a contingent of the luckless Jacobite army in l745 and later, more gingerly and erratically, by Sir Walter Scott in his carriage. Two, of the three hump backed bridges of the nineteenth century, survive from this past and effectively act as speed breaks as does, more noisily, the sheep grid across the crown of the road at the top of the hill. On the river side, the new beech plantation gives the odd glimpse downwards, through the trees to the curving river, and the angular pattern of the lambing fields, with the house very firmly

The Old Plantation is entered from the drive and along this short walk of Spanish chestnuts, planted in 1984, with a carpet of fallen leaves.

The stone and slate shed used for storing the wool clip and dipping equipment in the past.

in the middle distance of the picture. To the careful and wakeful driver, solicitous of his car on the steel bars of the grid, the valley still unfolds almost regally before him and sweeps eastward to the pass at the other end.

Rather like the old shelter belt, the existing garden was a ruin of a similar nineteenth century date and probably part of the Gibson regime. It was the poor relation to the histrionics of the valley, feeble in its conventionality, and not very convincing. It was little more than a quarter of an acre, taken from the field between the house and river, and sloped eastwards with the lower part, beneath the periphery beeches, a frost pocket. Not too long ago, an attempt had been made to remedy this by amputating their lower boughs and letting in more light that left the three trees heavily lopsided. The long rectangle of the garden was cut into at the top with a wide gravel path that led from the yard, on the other side, to a front door on this side. It was all ridiculously pretentious and impractical, and I doubt if it was ever used. It went as soon as I gained possession. One of the lateral garden walls had been smashed by a sycamore in a violent storm in the sixties and the sheep had happily moved in through the gap and left little that was green. What did remain were the upper parts of a privet hedge, box edging and some rambling roses, red and white, all of which I have kept. The rest was nettles with wild raspberries in abundance.

As far as I could tell, when the garden was carved out of the field, the immediate area was planted in an ornamental fashion with sycamore, elm and horse-chestnut linking them up to those on the boundaries of the field. This appeared as a small, decorative patch in the bigger quilt of the valley and appeared as such in the Ordnance Survey of 1899. It also had, to my eye, a curiously eighteenth century air – a house and walled garden set in a park but all done on a miniature scale. It reminded me of some of the West Highland manses of the early nineteenth century with their glebe fields and stable buildings that we had looked at exhaustively before coming here. The first improvement then was to integrate the house with its new woodland setting, to reduce the visual conflict between the old and new landscapes and the contrasting ways of life they represented.

On the other side of the house from the garden was a rather rushy field of about an acre that ran uphill to the road with the Old Plantation to one side and the sheep fanks to the other. It was also the path our water supply followed, running underground and downhill to the house from the well on the other side of the road. This effectively limited the planting of deep rooted trees anywhere in its vicinity. A rickety fence of slack wire and less than vertical stobs, barely stock proof, ran along the roadside and gave an immediate and correct impression of dilapidation and neglect. It was one of the first things I removed and replaced it with a new dyke, built by a retired shepherd, rather bent and bespectacled, to whom I acted as barrowman. He cannibalized the necessary stone from old walls that had been incorporated into the new forest and reinvented them along the roadside. It was my first lesson in drystane dyking and a remarkable experience. Behind this wall, and at a safe distance from the water supply pipe, I planted Scots pine, the spry descendants of the inhabitants of the Old Plantation, who would help to lessen its stark isolation. The wet ground was extremely acid with a high Ph factor, suitable for pines, but not much else, and even they had to be mound planted. They had as well the unfortunate habit of loosing their lateral branches much earlier than they should, so that they looked like triangular lollypops. The only way around such disadvantages was to introduce the rhododendron as under planting, even though the

ABOVE The raw material used for both house walls and dykes in an outcrop on the hillside above the house.

ABOVE RIGHT A modern, reconstructed dyke showing too many small stones and little top weight given by the capstones.

RIGHT A traditional dyke, probably early nineteenth century, showing the small and smooth lower part with through stones and loosely piled capstones, found throughout the valley.

rampant, purple *ponticum,* or large hybrids with spotty flower heads, had little appeal and suggested some doleful highland shooting lodge. The alternative was to try the species, which would present a challenge both for them and me, and give an appealing sense of botanical history. I felt that they might put me in touch with the collectors like Hooker, Forest and Kingdon Ward, or rhododendron gardeners like Osgood Mackenzie or Sir James Horlick at Gigha: it was an intoxicating sensation, a compound of vanity and realism. But to get anywhere in this august botanical line, I needed more shelter from frost and wind than the new dyke and the infant pines would provide. I had, too, the idea that I could treat this area as a self-contained garden, tucked away in the same way as the small walled garden below the house, one with a formal character and the other, the rhododendron, a more romantic one.

I protected this putative garden from the prevailing western wind with a beech hedge on the dry ground at one end and beside the erstwhile track to the house. I intended to keep this hedge to wall height, that is about 4 feet, but the wind hopped over this with ease and so the top was raised to 7. The Old Plantation offered shelter after a fashion from the north but the area was largely open and light from the east. The date for this was 1980 when, as luck would have it, I joined the National Trust for Scotland's garden committee that did two things for me, both pleasant. I was catapulted into a small group, usually about eight or so, of knowledgeable gardeners who undertook a spirited, annual tour of the gardens in the Trust's possession and wrote polite reports on what they found. As a casual and not very perceptive visitor in the past, this regime took me where I would probably not have gone, and certainly not in such company, for the committee included at least two rhododendron experts, one of whom ran the great rhododendron nursery at Glendoick in Perthshire. In this way, I could see what I wanted, be warned of the pitfalls, hear how perfection could be achieved and given the means to find it: marvelous.

The key was shelter and if I was wise, it was suggested, I should start with the hardiest and no doubt dullest of plants, for cold and wind were as bad here as in any Highland garden: I was after all in marginal territory. So it was a case of a dreary slog for the first five years, certainly with rhododendrons in the H4 group, 'hardy anywhere in the British Isles', as Hillier reassuringly put it. So I duly planted, behind the infant pines to the west, *Rhododendron ponticum*, its sport 'Cunningham's White' and *R. catawbiense.* They grew but surprisingly slowly, were easily outpaced by the neighboring pines and produced

Half way down the former track
and looking up to the gate with
beech hedge to one side and
branches of a *Sequoia sempervirens*
on the other.

extremely wishy-washy flowers. The scene resembled some sort of battlefield, after the armies had moved on, if the photos of the Somme were anything to go by. I then tried, via Glendoick, some ponticum that came directly from Turkish seed and they grew better and produced a strongly coloured flower and succulent leaf quite unlike its beaten up, corrugated cousins. At this stage too, it was clear that the plants along the roadside should be pollution hardy and I was recommended a hybrid for this, a versatile one called 'Christmas Cheer' that might, with some luck, flower in January even with me. It has done this. Hatred of carbon monoxide was quickly apparent on the leaves of *R. lanatum*, which I planted near the road in an appropriate boggy spot, but *mallotum* and *hookeri* did not seem to mind though they were reluctant to appear above the dyke. I also set amongst them, for scale, some field maple and dog roses, which would also prosper in such a position and give an informal hedgerow affect, for I was keen not to draw attention to the garden.

At this point, and in this part of the garden, there was little to do but wait and make sure that my fences were sheep and goat proof. Deer have never been a serious problem around here, though the forest contains enough roe to provide sport for a shooting syndicate, curiously led by Mr Gunn. So, after five years I might modestly start my species garden. I tried as well to stay within the H4 category and planted so that I might have a long flowering season, from January to July, all being well, starting with *R. dauricum* and *mucronulatum* (this doing particularly well from the start), *R. pseudoyanthinum, R. campylocarpum* (slower than I thought and needing more shelter). I was also keen on the scented kind and *R. fortunei* was a great success as was *R. decorum*. A little later I tried *R. auriculatum* which has grown well but only flowered once and when it does again I doubt if I will see though I may smell it at 12 feet. My further weakness was for the large leaved rhododendrons that I had seen growing spectacularly at Inverewe and Brodick Castle on the isle of Arran and on which the Trust committee usually doted. I planted *R. rex* in 1985 and then *R. falconeri, sinofalconeri* and *R. sinogrande* in the 1990s: none have flowered but they have produced their 50 cm leaves pretty well unscathed. By 2000, the garden had about forty species, growing more or less happily, with some disappearing jungle-like into the pines. In assembling them, apart from a fondness for yellow, I have favoured those with interesting leaves or smell over colour and, in this way, the garden is a deliberate alternative to that beside the house. As a contrast too, the house garden is a walled and structured affair, whereas the rhododendron one has little shape except for a roughly triangular pattern of paths set within its boundaries. I doubt if it counts as a wild garden for it lacks both sufficient variety, beyond the hackneyed primroses and bluebells, and artlessness of the Gertrude Jekyll sort. Neither is it in any way a botanical garden, in the instructive sense of Loudon and his *Gardener's Magazine*, nor a plantsman's garden. Instead, it edges towards an odd, hybrid form without apparent

The drive turns at this point and passes the small porch to enter the long yard with a beech, *Fagus* 'Riversii', framed against the house double gable.

structure or any commanding presence, best described, unenthusiastically, objectively and knowledgeably as an overgrown shelter belt in the shooting lodge style.

Like so many things in gardening, cost and labour are constraints. I put a break on acquiring more than six rhododendrons a year, to which I have more or less stuck, and over this twenty year period the cost has risen from about £80 to around £120. My proscriptive H4 steered me away from expensive exotics and I have tried to collect my plants from Glendoick, if I possibly could, feeling, irrationally, that relatives would tolerate each other better. I liked to buy small plants, for they needed less shelter and recovered from the shock of exposure faster, though the death rate was still high. All the protection I offered them was a mantling of decaying bracken, which I had in plenty, and a bit of weeding around the roots from time to time. Later, I latched on to the idea of internal hurdles, irregular barriers of broken tree branches and the like that acted as secondary windbreaks, to about 3 feet. No doubt all of this sounds pretty small beer, but I was single handed and had a fair number of calls on my time even within the garden. Occasionally, I had recourse to child labour (mine) but this proved to be more trouble than it was worth and surprisingly expensive. I have operated a similar policy of fiscal prudence with the bulbs I have planted in the rough grass below the rhododendron garden and along the short drive, formerly track. Again, I spent about

The yard from the north end with a simple pattern of walls, stones and grass, not much changed since the eighteenth century.

£100 per year on daffodil bulbs (mice or voles eat everything else except snowdrops) of which the traditional Lent lilies (*Narcissi lobularis*) and Tenby daffodils (*N. obvallaris*) have naturalized and spread well, running downhill to the damper ground. Their height is in their favour, about 4 inches, for the wind is unkind to their taller and later daffodil companions.

In front of the house, edging the yard, are now two small lawns of which the larger has a hawthorn hedge, cut late so that it can flower, which continues where the more formal beech hedge left off. It screens the bottom of the Old Plantation and has hybrid larch planted behind it. The overall effect is to give height to the strong horizontal lines of the various outbuildings. These are very simple and plain with their own rugged character for I have kept them clear of vegetation and softness, and it is only where the adjoining house meets the garden that I have planted, as a transition cover, ivy, of several sorts, cotoneaster and *Hydrangea petiolaris*, all needing rigorous control. On either side of the garden gate, I have established two yews that I have kept to the height of the wall, just above 4 feet, and of about similar width, so they look rather like a couple of green sentry boxes for officious dwarfs. They control entry to what is playfully termed, Finlay-like, the ante- or anti-garden, a sort of pausing place before the real thing.

The interlude is short: a small space with a central grass path bordered by box with, on the field side, three laburnum, *anagyroides*

RIGHT At the house with the white gate into the ante-garden between two clipped yews as sentry boxes and before the laburnums come into leaf.

OPPOSITE LEFT A stone medieval head, probably Scottish and from a demolished Tolboth, on the wall of the ante-garden and seen through the branches of *Rosa multiflora*.

OPPOSITE RIGHT A companion head also on the wall of the gable wall of the ante-garden.

'Autumnale', *alpinum* and 'Vossii', with an under planting of *Ribes aureum*, and on the other side a rather unsuccessful group of rugosas (not enough light in high summer) with an espalied laburnum on the house wall. I have also, climbing through the trees, the over-vigorous *Rosa villosa* 'Wedding Day' with, at the gate end, *R. rubrifolia* and *multiflora*, host to a late honeysuckle and *Clematis flammula*. Peering out from this tangle are two stone heads, probably late sixteenth century, with blind eyes and lolling tongues, perhaps from some demolished Scottish Tolboth, which I bought at auction in 1992. They are on brackets (I take them in each winter), and they seem to stare myopically at the visitor going under the laburnum tunnel in a half bent position as though genuflecting to the garden's god. There are a further two yews at the end of the passage, clipped to the same form as the entrance pair, so this little garden can be read as either the beginning or the end.

As I have written, the garden was here when we came. The original shape was a long rectangle with the house closing one side and stone dykes the other three. It is now divided by a privet and yew hedge into an upper and lower garden for there is a steep fall to the river. In all, there is less than quarter of an acre, not much more than the average back garden to a terrace house. There were two principles, if that is not

too strong a word, which guided what I have done. Ruthlessly, there are no herbaceous plants, too much work, and a colour limitation to white and yellow, and of course green, all of which have tended to concentrate the mind. Beyond this and in my imagination, there hovered an image of a walled formal garden, neglected and gone to seed and now thoroughly romantic in its disarray and uncontrolled exuberance. I had seen plenty of those sad places at first hand in my childhood during the late forties and I had read *The Secret Garden* with its romantic account of the walled garden at Misselthwaite Manor. I sought something of this Hodgson Burnett kind of schadenfreude, a haunting melancholy that tempered too much zeal.

As the garden was on a slope, it was comparatively dry, though one side, the west, was considerably damper and deeper than the other. Around it, there were a fair number of large trees, three beeches at the bottom, a large Scotch elm to the east and a mixture of chestnut, elm and sycamore, as shelter from the prevailing wind from the south west, with the odd stump, like a scalp, showing what could be done when it was in earnest. The soil was what might be expected on a hillside, stony, about 6 inches of topsoil, and rather sandy with the better ground at the bottom and west side, but not overly acid for once. The garden had also a slight tendency to be a frost pocket and this became

ABOVE Looking towards the house from the new beech avenue, planted in stages from 1985, with the field in a strong green flush of high summer.

RIGHT A similar view but a decade earlier with the house unpainted and the hills unplanted.

OPPOSITE ABOVE The top of the four-faced sundial of carved sandstone with the dials placed aesthetically rather than correctly and the gnomon reading wrong.

OPPOSITE BELOW A grotesque lion's head, possibly seventeenth century, in sandstone that sits on the dyke beside the little, white gate to the field.

more apparent as it established its own microclimate, several degrees warmer than the other side of the house and rhododendron garden. That said, the temperature could regularly go down to ten degrees below freezing in January and produce a stark reminder that this was marginal gardening. Winter flowering plants like *Jasminum nudiflorum* or *Viburnum bodnantense* were safe, early spring *Clematis montana* or *armandii* in danger.

The house sat at the top of the garden facing south east, looking down and across the field towards the river that could be heard but not seen. It set the scale. The garden door, two bays from one side and four from the other, was off centre and the axis from it ran not quite straight to the four-faced sundial at the bottom. Where it passed through the original privet hedge, I had planted two yews that were to join and make an archway with a wide pedimented top. On either side and facing the house, I cut two round headed niches to take a pair of guardant lions on plain sandstone plinths, Leo and Cleo, which had come from my parents' garden. This rather ambitious piece of garden architecture echoed the house on a reduced scale and firmly established the formal and classical element to the garden. Its source was the much grander and more elaborate Physic Garden gateway, of 1632, by Nicholas Stone in Oxford. But unlike Stone, I had little control over my green material and though the yews had both come from Hilliers at the same time, 1975, perversely they grew at different paces and in different tones of green, more noticeable at some times of the year than others, but always eagerly remarked upon. In front of the arch, a small lawn ran gently down from the house with, on either side, a low hedge of box that formed two borders where I practiced my colour scheme.

I started with several large plants to give scale and the basic colour of white. These were *Viburnum plicatum*, 'Lanarth' and 'Mariesii', to the east, and *Hydrangea sargentiana*, a variant of *H. dumicola* (from Kiftsgate), and *Viburnum bodnantense* 'Dawn', which is white, on the damper west. On this side, as a transition to the chestnut and sycamore trees beyond, I planted a yellow Cornelian cherry and *Amelanchier canadensis* with, as a vertical stop at the privet end, a *Calocedrus decurrens* with a Russian vine slowly making its way up the light side. In winter, when the leaves are gone on the chestnut and sycamores, this border is very exposed, so I have heightened the wall by growing a yew up against it and so added a few extra feet in shelter height with, at its feet, its relation the plum-fruited yew, *Podocarpus andinus*. Into this, I have mixed more roses than I probably should have for this is hardly

rose country even in Scotland. On either side of the yew arch and leaning into it, I have an immensely sweet smelling 'Madame Legras de St Germain', an alba, with tissue paper petals and small neat leaves, which never gets beyond 6 feet in height, more than can be said for the 'Kiftsgate' rose. This is now covering the tops of cherry and amelanchier and on the way to the laburnums where it can fight it out in an airborne battle with 'Wedding Day'. To balance such excessive white, I established several yellow leaved shrubs, a *Philadelphus coronarius* 'Aureus', a fern-leaved guelder rose and *Weigela middendorffiana,* whose washed out yellow flowers are relatively insignificant. So the overall scheme has remained true to the papal colours, so much so that I went as far as to plant a Japanese cherry, *Prunus* 'Yukon', which promised and delivered 'pale yellowish, tinged green' flowers, as Hilliers accurately put it. About all these plants and trees, there is the romantic abundance of Misselthwaite Manor, perhaps emphasized by the various honeysuckles and clematis that wend in and out amongst the viburnums for much of the summer and a feeling of the wild suggested by a yellow leaved *Rubus cockburnianus,* whose vigorous shoots break the order of the box hedging with abandon. It is here that the inevitable serpent in the garden appears – *Prunus* 'Tai Haku', the great white cherry, which after 6 feet has grown vigorously, horizontally and inwardly, casting destruction with its shade. I am fearful of pruning on the scale needed and have contented myself with its spring beauty and the asymmetry that upsets the rectangle.

After about fifteen years, that would be around 1987, this tree first suggested that the garden had become rather too restrictive and prescriptive, and the effect perhaps conventional. I had also read Robin Lane Fox's *Better Gardening,* which made me look again and askance at my planting in a somewhat Nancy Mitfordish fashion. To make life more exciting for the plants and myself, I put in a *Magnolia wilsonii* and a *Eucryphia* × *intermedia,* one to the east the other west, and crossed my fingers. I am now at my second *wilsonii,* the first carried off in a late frost in 1997, and disturbed by the sudden reduction of shelter over the garden dyke through elm disease. In fact, the whole business of shelter has become a changing factor. The surrounding trees keep out the south west wind in summer and break cold winds, but, the more efficient they are the less light they allow in. This has turned the east facing border into a darker one than I would have wished, especially for summer flowering plants. I have partially solved such difficulties by growing one plant through another and the *Prunus* 'Tai

Haku', prudently bending from the wind, supports and holds up to the light a yellow lilac and *Leycesteria formosa* by its branches in this way. But I fear that sooner or later, after some spectacular death, the whole border will have to be replanted. When this happens, I should give more thought to the garden time table, for though winter has jasmine, *Daphne mezereum*, viburnums and the yellow Cornelian cherry, with an underplanting of snowdrops, autumn has little after the end of the buddleias and hydrangeas, because of my floral exclusion policy. This season produces, in most years, little but the gentlest of colour, apart from the creeper on the house and fothergilla leaves, for it is never dry or still long enough for this to happen successfully. I have to be content with brown leaves and then none, for even the privet moults.

If I look at the house from under the yew arch, I see a plain and rather too architectural façade of busy astragalled windows and long, flat walls. I have tried to do something about this by making three buttresses, two on either side of the garden door, a clipped *Escallonia* 'Donard Seedling' and a *Cotoneaster conspicuus*, and the third from one of the yews of the ante-garden. All three project forward about 4 feet and have sloped tops that let in light to the lower branches. They are repeated in flat form by two golden hops, twining through white roses and a virginia creeper and so filling the end bays on either side of the garden front. In winter, much of this is covered by winter jasmine and there is a footing along the base of the wall of *Cotoneaster horizontalis* that shelters the roots of honeysuckles and *Clematis orientalis*. The wall itself is painted white, so the planting conforms to yellow and green. To give a little exoticism, and a perhaps misguided whiff of the south, I have blue agapanthus hybrids and white lilies in largish pots whose heads can be seen from the windows when looking out in high summer.

Turning at the yew arch, and looking down rather than up the garden, gives a rather dispiriting view of the fruit garden. Once again, I have planted smallish fruit trees to give perspective to the three large beeches that stand at the bottom just over the garden wall and to hopefully signal the arrival of spring amongst the fruit. One of these, a red leaved plum, makes a good foil to the hydrangea and Russian vine on the calocedrus on the other side of the dividing hedge. A grass path edged with box in poorish health has white, red and black currants to one side with plum trees to the other and gooseberries at the bottom. At the very bottom of the path, off-axis with the centre of the house, is a four-faced sundial, initialed and dated 1735, that I have on a sandstone plinth about 4 feet high. At the base is a planting of yellow

The four-faced pedestal sundial of 1735 in a planting of yellow day lilies and *Alchemillia mollis* with ivy on the wall behind.

day lilies and the invasive *Alchemilla mollis*, fine in summer but a rather dismal bundle in winter. In all of the garden, this is probably the area the Gibsons would recognize and appreciate my berries, especially the gooseberries, mould free and vigorous, even if they disapproved of my rough grass setting for the fruit trees, nearly hiding their treasured rhubarb of the champagne sort. This is not Peter Rabbit country and, I fear, the new apple orchard has stolen its thunder and my attention: it has become, as it were, the apple of my eye.

I wonder if fifteen trees constitute an orchard? This one has less than a quarter of an acre and is just beyond the gate at the bottom of the yard, set on a rise with the end of the Old Plantation to the north. It runs south in two terraces formed from the retaining walls for a large, corrugated iron barn, put up around 1946, when such structures were sold off by the army. It was used for hay, and when haying was given up, for wintering sheep, with the result that the topsoil was well manured. In its peeling red paint and rusting doors, it was an eyecatcher that no self-respecting improver would contemplate for long. Sad to say, I only got rid of it in 1986: delayed through indecision. I replaced it with a small boathouse, with a slate roof, on part of the site, put two espaliered apples, 'Reinette d'Orléans' and 'Worcester Pearmain', on the south east wall, and then after coming across a nurseryman in 2002 who specialized in Scottish apples, set to. On the lower terrace I put in cookers, two of which, called 'Melrose White', had originated in the medieval abbey of that name and they appealed enormously to my sense of the past. On the upper terrace, I have a union of Scottish and English, cohabitating peacefully as far as I can tell, 'Lord Lambourne' with 'Scotch Bridget', and this has included 'Coul Blush', the most northern apple found in Scotland. These are early days to say I will regularly have apples as well as blossom, for this is a far cry from Scottish apple country. I keep the grass rough cut and in the bottom slope, towards the river, I have planted Tenby daffodils and left it at that.

Surrounding all this on three sides and giving the garden its setting and shelter, is a large walled field of about three acres that has the remains of its original planting of sycamores and later beeches. It stretches from the road to the river and is of a roughly circular shape and takes in the sheep fanks. I saw here the opportunity to make a sort of Capability Brown landscape where he had converted a formal landscape into an informal one, with the examples of Burton Constable or Blenheim distantly in mind. I wished to hide the house from the road in summer, with only a short avenue giving a view to the hills from the south facing windows of the house. I planted this double line with a mixture of beech and sycamore and the odd lime, a sort of patchwork effect to suggest trial and error. I related them to the trees scattered over the field, so that it seemed that there had been a formal landscape of avenues and vistas that was later clumped in the eighteen century style. I transplanted one of two large trees, following Steuart's *The Planter's Guide* to give, as he recommended, an instant landscape. This was an expensive and risky enterprise and one really only to be undertaken on a large scale to be effective, as a real improver would have understood at the outset. I thickened the planting around the periphery of the field, filling in where elm disease had struck in the nineties, leaving me with only one large Scotch elm to the north. Isolated though the field was, the disease had come with leaves floating down the river and the trees died from the river inwards. I also increased the shelter to the garden side, largely with beech, and then

At the far end of the yard looking back towards the house and through a gate, companion to the drive one, with birch and alders to one side and a reconstructed garage of l985 on the other.

scattered specimen trees, walnut, Indian chestnut, Turkey oak, Spanish chestnut, and added the conifers of wellingtonia and cedar to the few, existing Scots pine. The last have become quite essential for the winter landscape and make a good contrast with the crooked umbrellas of the mature pines. They have all grown, or died, at an uneven rate and so give a more historical air to the landscape than I would have expected, though I feel that this disingenuous interpretation may be taken as an excuse by silviculturalists, but appreciated by the marginalists. Looking over it of an evening or walking through to watch the Soay lambs that graze there, the feeling of smug satisfaction is tempered with the chilling thought that it could be all a bit Pooterish.

I am not a great naturalist and have difficulty in seeing man as the fellow inhabitant of rabbits, frogs and deer, not better but just bigger. My excursion into such a world has been sheep. This is a sheep farm with a conventional flock of the blackfaced, about a thousand breeding ewes, mostly out of my control. But the flock of Soays, about twenty to

The field side of the yard steading with a central door opening from the byre into the field with on the extreme right the last of the original elms.

twenty-five, was my particular concern. I bought a nucleus of six in 1974 to graze the round field on the understanding that they were self-sufficient; they lambed and moulted (no tiresome shearing) without help, needed little winter feeding, and were best left alone. They would keep the grass under control. They were tough and lean and their meat dark and gamey and rather disagreeable. They were the original sheep of the mouflon type, dark brown with a light tan underbelly and legs, with short tails, found in the Celtic world before the Romans arrived with their improved breeds and pushed these remarkable animals into the highlands and islands of western Scotland, to fare as they could. It was Whisky Galore country and hence their name from the rocky island of Soay, depopulated in the 1930s. They were extraordinarily independent and lived in a cycle of their own and, if not overfed, were small and delicate, unlike the brash blackface or cheviots, and fitted in well with my diminutive park landscape. Their only fault was a deep love of trees, especially the trunk of a new and expensive one.

So much then for the domestic landscape: it has been one of continual and deliberate contrast, formal with informal, romantic and classical, small and large perspectives, a lot of work, little maintenance. As in much else, Henry Steuart has cheered me with his rare, comforting opinion – 'there is no situation so utterly hopeless, as not to be capable of considerable beauty, from wood planted abundantly and luxuriously'. Such utter hopelessness acted as a spur, possibly as Steuart may have intended, to produce a kind of creative chaos, the sort that has kept both garden and gardener on their toes.

The House

The garden and eastern side of the house with the garden door in a porch of escallonia and *Cotoneaster conspicuus* and a dramatic show from the golden hop, *Humulus lupulus* 'Aureus'.

Most garden books are properly about gardens but often too include the garden's setting in a landscape. It is less common for such books to concern themselves with the house that has its own broad category of literature. Such limitations are not from any lack of imagination or knowledge on the author's part, they are more a question of focus. As I have suggested in my preface, when I started here I had a very clear idea that I wished to develop or improve all three, house, garden and landscape, together and following roughly similar principles. It was an idea that the Romantic poets, like Wordsworth and Coleridge, had recognized when they asked cynically that the house belong to the country, not the country to the house. Although the practical problems of putting together a house and a garden are very different, they are paradoxically much the same, for each deals with space, colour, texture and so on. They are the setting for one another and give, in turn, each other meaning; for neither house nor garden can be an island 'entire of itself'.

At the start, I wrote critically of the bland garden accounts given by authors such as the anodyne Beverley Nichols. With house restoration there is a similar body of material, often quite serious, to which may be added the lifestyle sort, broader in scope and heavier on charm, best seen in the rumbustious tribulations of a year in Tuscany or Provence, full of sun and pastis. None of the last is found in the Scottish Borders, and my account of the house as part of a trilogy makes fairly sober and thoughtful reading. In such a partnership, the house must toe the line, established long ago by both setting and garden and heed the improver's concern for simplicity and modesty: the house either within or outside should never rise above its station.

In the classical past, any Roman household worth its salt had the appropriate family gods – the lar and penates – in the hall as the benign and watchful spirits of the household. The convention is an interesting one for it seems to give a face more human than the vague

A Roman stele of a farmer called Titianius, in costume with sickle and grapes in either hand, now one of the protective spirits of the house.

and aloof one of the genius of the place. I have two such forms that may fit such a bill and, hopefully, they will keep a vigilant and protective eye on what happens here. In the hall of the house, there is a small Roman stele (gravestone), from the classical province of Lydia in Western Turkey, which shows in high relief and diminutive form a Greek farmer called Titianius. He is carved in Roman costume with a sickle in one hand and a bunch of grapes in the other, making his occupation quite clear. He was probably a small farmer and a reasonably successful one too, perhaps a sort of Gibson figure, and is described conventionally in Greek as 'my very sweet father'. His counterpart is the rather grander figure of Sir Henry Steuart in the sitting room. As has been discussed, Steuart was the author of *The Planter's Guide,* which appeared in 1828 and ran to three editions with some influence on Olmstead and Central Park in New York. He was distinctly an improver, concerned with the successful and 'scientific'

Sir Henry Steuart, after the portrait by Sir Henry Raeburn, of circa 1815, which appeared as the frontispiece to his *The Planter's Guide* of 1843.

transplanting of large forest trees to create at a stroke a picturesque landscape. He practiced what he preached on some scale at his Allanton estate in Lanarkshire, now more or less obliterated. His reputation suffered, too, from his somewhat foolish genealogical and historical studies and Sir Walter Scott's poor opinion. After visiting him and Allanton, Scott condescendingly wrote that 'he had put me out of conceat with any profession of landscape gardener, now I see so few brains are necessary for such a stock in trade'.

The two would have made an odd pair and not only in historical terms. Steuart expected praise, Titianus probably did not: Steuart was a touchy aesthete and Titianius, as far as I can guess, an eminently practical soul, but both were devoted to making things grow quickly and on that level would have easily understood one another. Both would surely have felt, after looking around them, that I badly needed any divine help they could offer.

The house and farm were laid out in the l760s by the then Earl of Hopetoun, who was running the estates of his enfeebled cousin the Marquess of Annandale. This is documented by a map of the valley of around that time where the house is marked with a stylized rectangle and the inscription 'store farm', which simply meant sheep farm. A rather beaten George 11 penny of 1757 was found under the floorboards of the house and this suggests the early, rather than late, l760s. It was one of seven farms strung along the road and part of the estate, and was probably the poorest, as well as the most recently improved, for some of my neighbours were comparatively grand. It was not the first building on the site for there may well have been a medieval house nearby. The name appeared as a territorial title in the fourteenth century and the remains of what could have been the farmhouse of that time are apparent west of the house and near a source of water. Hillside burns were always the key to the position of all the farmhouses in the valley and the eighteenth century house was set beside a well that functioned domestically into the last century. It may have been the reliability of this water supply that encouraged the move eastwards by about a hundred yards, and a little lower, to a more sheltered spot. The new building was a long rectangle, one room deep, and running parallel to the river with the steading of stable and byre continuous to the east. Its design was simple and traditional and it perhaps only broke with convention in having an upstairs with some form of dormer window. The roof was slated and the walls were constructed from roughly coursed rubble and mortar that was then lime washed white. It seemed, at least to the Gibsons, sufficiently sophisticated for them to compare it favourably with the poverty of the cottages and farmhouses they had passed by on their jaunt to Kirkbean. The steading was of exactly the same material and colour. The overall effect must have been of some small blob, white fringed with green, overwhelmed by the vastness and greyness of the open landscape of hills and sky. The only description I know of this is a late one, of l957, where it was seen as a neat white house with, at the gate, a notice saying tersely 'cigarettes sold here'.

At some point in the later nineteenth century the roof was raised, new dormer windows set into it, the chimneys heightened and changed from stone to brick. However, in frugal style, the original chimneys remained below the roofline in the attic. At this time too, the house was divided, with the eastern end given a new staircase and kitchen to be used as a sort of bothy for a shepherd at the centre of the valley, with another in the cottage, Birkhill, the home of the Boa family at the head of the valley. Then, around 1927, a kitchen and storerooms with a large bedroom above were added at right angles to the roadside front and formed a small, cobbled entrance from the yard. It was carried out in brick in a rather shoddy fashion by a local building firm from Lochmaben. After that, time stood still as farming fell into depression, farm incomes followed and farm labour shrank. This was slowly apparent in the reduction of what was done. The horses, originally two, went, and the need to make summer hay for them, never easy, was discontinued altogether. Shepherding also suffered, the various hefts (sheep grazing patterns) were no longer moved around and the stells to hold them overnight allowed to fall into disrepair, and the higher ground casually or rarely grazed. Such a decline was obvious in the house, as well, where several of the upstairs rooms were not needed and, downstairs, the kitchen and scullery were the only ones in regular use and heated. The writing was already on the wall when the naturalist author of *Galloway and the Borders* lodged here in the 1950s while carrying out research on the ravens and peregrines. He wrote nostalgically that he spent 'some of the happiest days of my life, wandering over lonely uplands where the only souls I ever saw were other shepherds and returning at night to wonderful suppers and good talk'. As well as a writer, he was an equally sensitive photographer and took plenty of photographs of the valley before the green tide of afforestation swept in, a few of which he reproduced in his book. The end came in 1964 when the farm was sold, much of the land taken over by the Forestry Commission and the farming couple departed. And, as I have written, the sheep moved in.

The interior of the house we acquired was a fair example of the popular decorative styles of the last fifty or so years. Woodwork was brown varnished or stained, wallpaper deep colours with plenty of pattern, fern leaves a favourite, linoleum on floors of wood and concrete, and four pane windows. Fortunately, lack of money made up for any lack of taste and, beneath the grime and damp, parts of the original house survived, showing what had been there, and establishing the doleful character of the interior. Only one of the original six-paneled door remained downstairs, some of the window shutters and there were a further two upstairs, as well as the original wide, 10 inch, floor boards. But these were minor artifacts compared to the surviving and sophisticated wooden staircase, which curved slimly and elegantly from ground to bedroom floor in the centre of house, with a small hall to itself. It has been described professionally as 'a tight geometrical stair', and its source was not difficult to find. In

Looking down the main, wooden staircase of the mid-eighteenth century that curves sharply from the small garden hall to the bedroom floor.

the heyday of estate improvements, John Adam, elder brother of Robert, built, in 1762, a very grand factor's house in the centre of Moffat. It contained a curving staircase – our prototype – and presumably the joiners who worked on it later practiced their skills in other houses on the estate, hopefully with as much success as in our diminutive version. It was of course painted a deep brown, hiding the activities of wood beetle, and conforming to the general gloom of the interior. In all, it was not so much the case of Cinderella awaiting the prince, or some sort of Sleeping Beauty needing a kiss; such parallels would be going too far, it was more the ugly duckling needing understanding and a bit of feeding. Understanding was easy but feeding expensive, and it took the form of an immediate injection of cash to make the house wind and watertight and deal with the rampaging dry rot. There could be no question about the need for the improver: it was a question of sink or swim.

While the landscape needed a new balancing act between past and present, the garden sought revival and expansion; the house itself needed to return to its first simple forms and spaces. At the same time, attention had to be paid to its traditional surroundings, to capturing the patterns set out by the fields and garden as well as keeping the colours found there, much of which has already been discussed. It is clear that the tail that wagged the dog was, in this case, the garden setting, a reverse application of the usual garden room formula. With that said, it needed to be easily managed, like the garden, and reasonably comfortable according to the standards of the day, though I suspect that comfort had never been high in any list of my predecessors needs: not for them the evocative kitchen scene of labradors round the Aga. A certain Spartan dignity was closer to Gibson style and, for all that I know, of the lar Titianius. It was here that the commanding figure of historicism entered and just as quickly departed. I had little enthusiasm for the kind of National Trust interior that was dedicated to restoring a lifestyle gone by. I had seen enough of them. Nor was I keen on a Georgianisation or Victorianisation of the utilitarian, nor for that matter the archaeological style where the strata of the house was ruthlessly exposed. All seemed both silly and impractical. Ignored in all of this was the genius of the place, who seemed to have little worthwhile to say, and was indeed curiously tongue tied. As the exterior of the house was a basic exercise in simple geometry, it seemed best to follow the same architectural style in both house and garden, and let each reflect the broad principles of small scale and limited colour but strong shapes.

Certain things were quickly and easily done. Dry rot was eliminated or neutralized, the roof and flashings fixed, downstairs floor boards replaced with copies after the upstairs ones and shutters reinstalled. We had first electric then central heating with the pipes hidden in the walls and skirting radiators. The house was painted white inside and out and I relied on the contents to give colour and scale, using the rooms as spaces that opened into each other and gave long views in the garden border sense. In this, I was certainly influenced by those of Kettles Yard in Cambridge, which was being arranged by Jim Ede when I was there in the early sixties. It made a deep impression, if only as relief to the stuffy, antique style of so many of the College show rooms with their paneling and open roofs. This was strongly reinforced by the similar character of the Irish house of my parents-in-law, who had worked in this way but on a much grander scale and with much better contents in the 1950s. They had followed the genius of the place, almost in a literal fashion, by having rugs, curtains and some furniture made on the virtual doorstep, something sadly impossible in Scotland twenty years later. They then assembled in the house a collection of objects ranging from medieval to Miro and set them out in series of visual axes throughout the house with colour marking a turn to the left or right. The upshot was an interior of museum-like formality that formed a contrast, rather than a familiarity or sympathy, with the house's inexpressibly romantic setting.

At this point and looking back, I seem to have fallen into the trap of generality and avoided the discussion of cost. This has always been a determining factor and particularly so, as we were often dependent on public funds to meet some of our repair bills. As a very broken down, rural building of little architectural or historical consequence, it was possible to get funds up to £12,000 to bring the house to acceptable standards. These were not very high ones and excluded many of the basic capital costs like rebuilding the chimneys or renewing the roof and so on. Authority looked more favourably on rewiring or replumbing and the eradication of damp and dry rot. It was clear that, in their eyes, such steps were meant to be on the path leading towards a rustic bliss, healthy, warm and dry, but one that did not much appeal to my idiosyncratic liking for discomfort. The next infusion of funds, about five years later, was wholly mine. This was needed to pay for the running of the three rooms of the former bothy into the house and restoring it roughly to what it had been like before the nineteenth century alterations. This renovation involved cutting through stone walls, replacing rotten joist ends, renewing the floor boards and forming a bathroom to the bedroom upstairs. Ten years later, I started building again and this time on a more ambitious scale. Across the hall from the kitchen there was an ungainly addition of the 1920s of pantries and lavatory, all of which had developed dry rot and were ripe for demolition. I replaced them with a two storied gable that showed to the roadside a W shape in the Scottish rural tradition, and this gave that side of the house some badly needed character. I had my reservations about its character that seemed to have ended up, with its skew stones and astrigalled windows, close to a pastiche of the Georgian vernacular, as practiced by the grand old man of Scottish architecture, Sir Robert Lorimer. In fact, a guest went so far as to wittily claim it was Lorimerette.

I planted ivy to successfully mask the junction in the harling between old and new and time did the rest very quickly. It provided, just as importantly, a better planned downstairs with above a dressing room and large bathroom. In carrying out this work, I used a local architect, whom I hoped would prove more worldly wise than I was and keep the builders and plumbers to a rigorously imposed schedule. This, he more or less achieved, but, unfortunately revealed a greater familiarity and addiction to bureaucratic paper work than building and produced much better contract descriptions than architecture. These and he cost nearly £30,000 and exhausted my constructive genius and considerably calmed my improving instincts for the time being, as well as whispering about the wisdom of being your own master.

The simplest path is always the hardest to find and follow – true for both garden and house. There is a basic mood for both that must be recognized and captured at the start and, to my way of thinking, it should be more or less the same. My first impression was of uniform

A view of the sequence of white, lit spaces in the interior of the house with the renewed floorboards exaggerating the perspective.

decay and dereliction and that made such a relationship obvious. The dreary interior of brown varnish and damp, and an exterior of uniform battleship grey, were matched by the broken garden walls and the rioting nettles of the outside. The genius of such a place, it seemed, was some old man, unshaved, short-sighted and on a crutch. In starting to change things, it became obvious at once that small houses, like small gardens, need a simple pattern where more is less and each room could absorb only a certain amount of colour and limited shapes. It also helped that they could be seen as continuing spaces, opening into each other, rather than two or three separate, cube-like rooms: the hermetic room was a foe. Rather like the garden, I approached the interior as a series of perspectives with the vistas terminated by some arresting object, sculpture or painting, with the light from the windows making shapes on the plain floors to lead the eye smoothly along. The curved staircase – described by a neighbour, who had seen too many films with Scarlett O'Hara, as in the 'Gone with the Wind' style – did not fit any such pattern, for its emphasis was vertical rather than horizontal, an effect increased by the carpet runner and brass stair rods. In the way of Canova's larger than life Napoleon at Apsley House in London, I put an overlarge piece of Greek sculpture, in fact another stele, in the stairwell where the weight of the marble clashed satisfactorily with the domesticity of the thin stair balusters and the blank curing wall. It was just possible, standing under the yew arch of the garden, to see it through the glass garden door and on axis.

A more radical break with the past was made with the chimneys. Upstairs, the bedrooms had simple mid-Victorian iron grates that went well with the characters of the rooms, downstairs was a different matter. There, the chimneys of the three principal rooms had been progressively altered, with a Baxi back boiler in dark brown, glazed tiles in the dining room, the most recent and unfortunate. I replaced all three with ones from the early nineteenth century of the sort that the Gibsons might have installed had they had any surplus funds. The dining room one was a case of serendipity: I came across it after it had recently been salvaged from Brandon Street, on the edge of the Edinburgh New Town, and had just time for the builders to enlarge the Baxi opening for a neat fit – very. It was cast iron, in the gothic style of the early nineteenth century, and similar examples can be seen in London in what was the architect Sir John Soane's house, and now Museum. The other two were bought from the owner of Dunmore Park in Stirlingshire, who was selling bits and pieces of the unroofed

house from the doorstep to all who asked and paid. The house had been designed by William Wilkins, architect of the National Gallery, in l820, and the grander of the two chimneypieces, in dark grey marble with a brass inlaid grate, and came from 'Lord D's Room', according to the Wilkins plan. The other was a simple stone one, done with scagliola to resemble deepest porphyry. One went into the large sitting room, the other the smaller. The overall effect was to raise the style of the interior but still leave the rooms as simple spaces.

In connecting the garden and house in this fashion of views and vistas, it seemed possible to continue the site lines into the more distant landscape, with some sculpture at critical places. Such a pattern, had been the bread and butter of the eighteenth century landscape gardener and there were plenty of modern precedents, particularly in Scotland. Not too far away was Ian Hamilton Finlay's Little Sparta and, in the other direction, west into Galloway, was Glenkiln with the Henry Moores, Rodin and Epstein, and the land forms of Charles Jenck's at Portrack beside the river Nith, all of which could be placed in the garden category of High Art. However, I was hesitant, because I saw such sculptural forms as lessened by their setting where they were overpowered by the vast landscape the further they moved from the garden. I also felt that what evolved from the ground, or was shaped and constrained by it, fitted in well, like Jenck's spiraling grass hills, or the traditional cairn, but the odd punning piece of sculpture by Finlay or even Henry Moore's abstract figures did not. To me, they appeared little better than the kinetic pylons of the wind farms, like those found restlessly gyrating on the Cumbrian moors. Such sophisticated pieces of sculpture and their intellectually demanding response were better, and more at ease, in an informal garden setting, such as that of the Maeght Foundation at St. Paul de Vence in France, which risked putting Giacometti out of doors. Nowhere is this contrast seen better than in the great sculpture park of Storm King, outside New York and in the Hudson Valley, where the work of Serra and Noguchi succeed but Calder or di Suvero fail, for they seem like interlopers from a museum.

I would have liked to put some cairn-like form on the hilltops but few, thanks to the new forest, were easily visible from below. To be seen effectively, they needed to be huge, otherwise they might in the end look like some pimple on the great face of the hillside. The valley is composed of hills that have always immediately and forcibly caught

Looking out of the garden door to the yew arch with moisture rising from the lawn in a summer's morning.

the spectator's imagination as the patient, enduring hills of eternity. And standing in the house, they set the limit of the view and measured the long fingers of light. Nor did I wish to interfere or reduce by some tawdry badge of ownership their traditional and historical role as the stout bastions of freedom – a mood very strong in the Scottish consciousness. These hills, during the Covenanting period of the l670s, were the refuge for the persecuted religious and political dissidents, permanently on the run from the military of their oppressors. In the valley, several of the Covenanters, when found, were executed on the spot and so Watch Knowe, just above and to the west of the house, was used by them as a lookout where they waited for the alarming arrival of the dragoons. Of all the periods through which the house and its hills have passed, this, imaginatively, seems to have taken the greatest hold and set the enduring feeling of freedom and one where even the wind has been termed somewhat poetically 'the wind of God'.

Looking at the winter sleet from the dining room window towards the yew arch and the beeches at the bottom of the garden.

How Matters Stand

An almost aerial view of the valley looking out over the western hills with the river, house and fields on the flat bottom.

What I have written so far has fallen into the trap of generality, with little close attention paid to much for very long. In a sense, the whole has taken over from the parts with seemingly endless variations on the improvement theme. So I have reversed the order here and set out series of verbal walks along the more important axes. I have explained simply how these evolved and, with the camera, the roles of the significant plants and trees along the way. Looking back, it was in every instance a case of accepting what was there and seeking a sympathetic character from such, often daunting, physical circumstances. I have also tried, as far as I can, to avoid the garden tour that so often makes boring as well as smug reading and where all comes right in the end, rather like a pantomime.

It seems reasonable to start with the roadside gate, for first impressions are important: they set the tone of what is to be found beyond. In the past, and certainly in 1899, the track to the house simply left the public road and that was that. In such a landscape, the road cut through a large holding and gathering area for the sheep and was a tolerated inconvenience, for there was little traffic. Such certainly was the case with my next door neighbour, where the road divided house from farm steading in a long curve. I settled for a modern farm gate, tubular and painted white, with an 8 feet span between the dykes, on either side, that were of the same height. The local authority also insisted upon a bell mouth, a neutral area of the road where a car could wait or unload safely, in the end no bad idea. To give some prominence to the opening, I planted a few sycamore and a beech on one side. I continued the beech hedge up to and over the top of the wall on the other side with an ash and pines beyond, starting with the smaller *Pinus cembra*. I do not know how many arrivals contemplated the scene from this opening. A few were doubtless too distracted by trying to open the gate to take in much, but, if they did, the delphic message of practical simplicity was confounded by a road with no end in sight.

Looking from the gate to the beech
hedge following curve of the track,
now a modest, unsurfaced drive.

The old farm track I elevated to the status of drive rather
reluctantly. I could have had an agricultural grant to make it a
concreted surface or, alternatively, it could have been tarmacked. I
disliked one and the other was expensive and in the long run
impractical. I left it as it was, put down some stones and smoothed
the raised centre into a grassy serpentine line that snaked its way
down to the house with cut grass verges repeating the pattern. In
winter, the rain water makes two canals that run speedily downhill,
so I have a sunk cross drain at the bottom to stop the flow. It has a
pleasantly old-fashioned air that perhaps suggests the home of
Jemima Puddle-duck rather than Squire Headlong of Headlong Hall,
Potter rather than Peacock.

Around the corner and looking through an archway of the autumn limes to the window of the sitting room of house.

The drive, ex-track, is about a hundred yards long and goes downhill in two serpentine curves, one tighter than the other, in the eighteenth century tradition of the line of beauty. The effect is emphasized further by the two grass verges, and the planting follows this pattern with the beech hedge, about 7 feet high. Two wellingtonias converge at the first curve to close the view and give a sense of mystery. It is only after this point that part of the house comes into view, with the window of the small sitting room looking you more or less straight in the eye, before you move sideways into the yard. Such a manoeuvre is a reduction of the picturesque dictum that the house should never appear in full view until the climactic end is reached.

I have used the drive side conifers as visual staging posts, charting the drop down the hill and also making a play of their pyramidal form against the horizontal beech hedge. Where they converge, the hedge breaks and turns at right angles to form the entrance to the rhododendron garden across a small burn. To give sharpness to this turn, the beech has been reinforced unobtrusively with hornbeam that corner better. Below this, the conifers are replaced on both sides with limes, three on one side, five on the other, which now form arches or a tunnel until the final curve, and the beech hedge is succeeded by a lower, hawthorn one. For the sake of interest, I have varied the usual small leafed limes with those of *Tilia platyphyllos* and *tomentosa* whose growth pattern and flowering season are much the same. All of this serves as a backdrop to the daffodils that start in the spring with a modest show from the Lent lilies. Beyond the gate, they increase in volume and size to make a deep border in the rough grass in front of the house. They obviously reveal the introductory yellow and white colour scheme and I have tried to keep them in solid blocks of the two colours and to plant sorts that are not too high, for the spring winds are as cruel and forceful as ever. For this reason, there are large drifts of the Tenby daffodil, 4 inches high, all yellow and at the end of March. The daffodil family usually continues until the middle of May and, about a month later, the rough grass in which they shelter is then cut on a monthly basis with the last in September. They have naturalized well and, in the case of the Lent lilies, readily increased as they move downhill towards damper ground. Apart from them, there is a large clump of snowdrops but little else, for crocus and aconites are all eaten by the warlike and hungry voles or moles.

The arrival at anyone's door is always fraught. Unless it is familiar territory, the path from car to door is rarely a seeing one, for the view is usually blocked by the grinning host: it is at the gate where the visual entrance is effectively made. The cottage door and cottage paths, so beloved by the late nineteenth century illustrators of the Helen Allingham sort, are a distraction that should not under any circumstances steal the garden's thunder. With this in mind, I have a path of flagstones (culled from the sandstone shelves of the defunct dairy) with the cobbles of the yard to one side, and the small lawn to the other; the distance is short, interest nil and the gardener's heartbeat in neutral. If anything, I consider the yard and its enclosing buildings as a holding space, calm and controlled, allowing the tensions of the journey to subside, rather like a stone Zen garden.

The long steading building that forms one side of the yard and showing the undulating slate roof and ridge stones of the mid-eighteenth century. The gutters are of the twenty-first century.

The rectangular yard has the house at one end, buildings on two sides and the hawthorn hedge forming the fourth. The hedge height more or less repeats that of the surrounding walls. The colours are here the grey of the stones, blue-grey of the slate roofs and white of the house and yard buildings. It is a clear geometrical space, perhaps rather harsh seeming after the pyrotechnics of the drive down and provides the proverbial light at the end of the tunnel. It is a space, too, that acts as a cross-roads, with openings through the white gates to the river and bridge, to the garden and house, and to a vista that runs west through the field and up to the road and forest on the other side. Such a space changes comparatively little for the surrounding trees are all at its edges. The only real variations are in colour when the daffodils appear and the hawthorns come into leaf and bloom. In the autumn, whatever colour there should be comes from two maples, *Acer pensylvanicum* and *saccharum*, and a red oak, *Quercus rubra*, all in their infancy. Apart from that, there is the phenomenon of the slate roofs of the old byre. They were warped from the heat of the animals below, move a bit according to the rise and fall of the temperature and suggest, better than the leaves, the gentle passing of time. All of which I made the more obvious by replacing the later metal with sandstone ridge tiles, along the same lines and colour as the rest. The stone too is a better host to the various roof mosses.

Walking from the yard past the house and the martial yew, sentry boxes at the garden gate, there is a further small gate let into the wall that skirts the field. On the yard side of this dyke, I have planted two roses, *Rosa moyesii* and *virginiana* running through their near relation the wineberry, *Rubus phoenicolasius*, with in front a *Caragana aborescens* 'Pendula' supporting a wandering and intrusive honeysuckle, late 'Belgica'. I have also the Tibet rose here, *Rosa wardii*, which seems – alarmingly – almost perfectly at home. On the other side of the wall is a Sargent's cherry (second attempt) and then two hawthorn trees, one pink, the other red, both leaning away from the wind and into each others arms in a rather romantic fashion. These all form the foreground to a short beech avenue that runs uphill towards the sheep fanks and the road. This I have planted in piecemeal fashion. It originally contained a mixture of elms, which had to be replaced after they died haphazardly, with trees that were around 6 feet. They took very slowly. The alternative of transplanting larger forest trees, here, was a hazardous undertaking and an expensive one, for I do not have even the modern equivalent of Sir Henry Steuart's planting machine. However, despite its short-comings, it presents a good view from the guest room window over the hills to the more distant ones, in an endless and thoroughly Scottish take on rolling infinity in the D.Y. Cameron tradition. In May, the field beside the road has several large outcrops of bluebells, before the bracken gets up, and changes the mid-blue to sharp yellow-green.

The field immediately beside the house was formed from two that I ran together by removing the gate between them in 1977. About fifteen years later, I decided on a modified piece of land sculpture by turning the wall ends in different directions, one curved one way and the other in a sharp, acute angle in the other direction. Apart from the visual effect, they gave the sheep shelter from almost any wind that blew. They, also, suggested to the susceptible imagination something archaeological, possibly prehistoric, which helped to make sense of the nearby circular mound. The valley is filled with similar sites that were possibly fortlets or protective enclosures of the pre-Roman period and this one of about 15 yards with an entrance to the east may be one of them. It is also in a clear line with the setting winter solstice. Of course, it could be an old overturned stell and my interpretation may well be in the line with memorable scene from Scott's *The Antiquary,* where the newly discovered Roman fort turns out to be nothing more than a former farm midden. It would not be the first time this has happened, for the source of Scott's story was in a misunderstanding that took place near here in the 1730s, with the amateur antiquarian Sir John Clerk as the victim. It is puzzling too that outside, rather than inside, the mound are the stumps of what must have been a sheltering circle of Scots pines planted well before 1899. They perhaps suggest something even older for the circle, in the tradition of Celtic folklore, was the doorway from the human world to the other world.

The putative fortlet and the concave and convex walls are part of a landscape solution in the style of a Capability Brown commission, where he had the problem of incorporating an earlier and formal landscape into his composition. In such a scheme of things, the beech avenue is to be seen as the old element, and the scattering of specimen trees and thicker planting at the periphery, the informal hand, as it were, of Brown. True to such a spirit, I have added a few sycamore to the beech avenue, the better to tie them into a scattering of such trees as specimens, and added lime, walnut, oak and ash for good measure. The odd conifers – wellingtonia, cedar and swamp cypress – were all planted to continue the shapes of the few existing nineteenth century

One of the few stands of Scots pine that remain, probably mid-nineteenth century, and sheltering the house from the prevailing winds of the south west: Soay sheep at their base.

Scots pines. They are intended to be seen from the garden, especially in winter, when they stand out best as a fundamental part of the landscape. In the same spirit, I have planted a group of silver firs, mostly *Abies nordmanniana* and similar, beside the sheep fanks to deepen the perspective from the house. However, the Brown-like landscape is not quite as artless, or persuasive, or historic as I hope it seems, for in part the trees disguise the power and telephone poles before disappearing underground for the distance to the house. It is a practical element that Capability would certainly have taken in his stride with a more sophisticated solution than mine. Sir Henry Steuart, of course, would have simply transplanted the poles.

Looking along a grass path bordered by old box wood towards the sundial with fruit on either side, all below three beeches of the nineteenth century planting, with the autumn forest beyond.

The cedar from the field has its near counterpart in the narrow, vertical form of the *Calocedrus decurrens* in the garden that in turn is the green companion to the yew arch. Such a signaling system is a useful one, for I do not wish either the garden or field to harbour in isolation a clutch of exotics, as these non-Scottish trees are regrettably termed. It has lent, too, some formality to both scenes and added to the geometry of the buildings. This is most obvious in the strict relationship between the house and garden where the yew arch and the garden door repeat the idea of opening and both are closed – quite accidentally – by the rather off-axis of the pedestal sundial at the bottom of the garden. There is as well, the broader geometry of the garden as a rectangular enclosure with the garden elevation of the house at the top almost balanced by three mature, rather mutilated, beeches at the bottom of the slope. It was into this tight pattern that I introduced the yew arch. It acts as a pivot in density and solidity through its perennial, dark green leaves, comfortable, lively, reassuring, protective – the primal antique – on either side are the counterweights of the couchant and watchful lions.

All of this lies along the visual route followed when looking west from the yard. But if the path in the other direction is taken, that is down to the river, an entirely different landscape is proposed though the starting point is much the same. This is the familiar white metal gate, similar to that at the top of the drive and reassuringly domestic, set in a short dyke that runs between the two garages that were built by me in the early nineties in the style of the yard buildings. Each cost around four thousand. It opens over a small flat bridge, little more than 6 feet in its span, crossing the burn that comes from the rhododendron garden and runs downhill to the river. After this bridge, there is a pathway of about 6 feet wide with limes on either side, as a simplified version of the driveway, that leads to the large river bridge and passes, further over, my collection of apple trees – that is all fifteen. Between the limes, on the west facing side, I have planted *Azalea mollis* to deter any intruding sheep or deer, for the azalea is quite poisonous. In the rough grass I have again scattered daffodils, Lent lilies this time rather than Tenby, for the bulbs of the former are too big for the shallow soil. After them come the bluebells at the top beside the gate to the yard. The final approach to the bridge is through rough cut grass with rowans along the riverside, which gives a wide view eastwards up the river to the high pass at the closure of the valley.

Standing on the bridge, itself a sort of elevated, viewing platform, the panorama offered makes a bitter return to the harsh landscape of

On the river bridge, rebuilt in 1990, and looking downstream with the lambing fields to one side and the house sycamores on the other.

old. There is little shelter and the hillside has formed a tunnel that exaggerates both the sound and fury of the wind striking the hills and blowing back with equal violence. The land pattern is essentially a practical one. The bridge, which I rebuilt in 1990 and connects to the farm track from the other side of the Old Plantation, crosses the river to allow tractor or agrocat access to the walled fields on the other side. Along this side, there is in gentler fashion a riverside walk of sorts that follows the water up the valley and into the plantations and looks after itself through a wild covering of thyme, harebells, primroses and clover flowers. This ends at the watergate and then crosses the river on boulders brought down from the lower hillside to the other bank, where a tall, oak stile bestrides the fence, moved here from the Old Plantation. It is modeled after one at Little Sparta with, in place of the

The terminal point of the river walk is the oak stile, made in 2006, which marks the entrance to the eastern forest.

punning tag, the distances up and down from town to town, usefully and functionally carved on the hand rail. It was made in 2006, locally. As it is partially hidden by the plantation trees, it offers little visual distraction from the bridge, raised on rough stone abutments about 7 feet above the water surface, which holds the key to understanding the valley that it seems to dominate or at least control. It draws together the various bits of wood, oddments of trees and pathways and explains how they work and to what end. It suggests, almost militantly, that it is a working landscape that tries to earn its keep and demands respect.

All of this sounds much more upbeat than it probably should and enough to embolden the most modest or timid of improvers. The illustrations, too, verify or confirm for better or worse what has been

The view looking upstream from the bridge showing the naturalized remains of the bulwarks constructed in l995.

written. While a positive spirit is essential to encourage the move forward and a brand of optimism should always be on hand, the discrete shadow of failure lingers as an unaccounted force in any garden and is the darker side of any landscape. This, I suppose, accounts for anxiety as a creative force in the gardener's development. Where failure is publicly recognized, it is too often dismissed in the jaunty style of silly-me that fails to recognize its positive benefits and the unhelpful voice of the spirit of the place. There is much to be said for gardening by default. After all, any garden is essentially composed of survivors, there being few photographs of the dead. Finlay's Little Sparta perhaps comes close with its war memorial sculpture.

It is worth considering from such a complex point of view, the three conifers half way down the drive. They are sequoia, two wellingtonia and a *sempervirens* – the giants of California – and need more space than they have been given in this shallow, Scottish corner. I have explained their purpose. They have grown with a strong and reasonable tendency to branch out of the wind and so overwhelm and block the edge of the drive. Such an expansion cannot easily be coped with for there is the clipped beech hedge on the other side. In time, these lower branches will drop, exposing the handsome spongy bole of the tree, but, until then, getting up or down and past them will be difficult and the Californian solution of cutting a road through the trunk is not possible for at least a century. The Roads Department remedy of cutting the branches on one side is an ugly one that leaves the tree lopsided and at risk in high winds. At this point in hand wringing, I ruefully recall the ruthless improver's advice of always planting two and later selecting the better to grow on – an aesthetic variation of cruel to be kind. The trees will stay, the drive curve more freely and beech hedge step back to form some sort of niche – probably. I would consider all of this as a fair example of gardening by default, where I have failed to take positive action and settled instead for managing such weakness. There are other instances, such as that of the 'Tai Haku' cherry, which have led to a less dramatic confrontation. Their resolution will be important in the future of the garden for they will turn procrastination into design.

My outstanding failure that I have left to the end is a further aspect of this philosophy. Beside the walled garden, there was a small rectangle with privet hedges down two of the sides. I think it had been intended as an alternative garden for the bothy when the house had been divided internally during the two wars. It does not appear in the 1899 plan. My mistake here was to try and make it fulfil two roles, first as the high and coloured background to the shrub border on the other side of the garden wall, second as a small formal bed around a baluster sundial. The latter, a rectangle edged with home grown box and filled with yellow roses and day lilies, like a piece of a parterre, worked well until the trees of my coloured background grew too high. Foolishly, I had planted as the centre a *pseudoplatanus* f. *purpureum* that I assumed would grow small and slowly, because of its exposure to the deadly east winds, a reasonable piece of negative gardening, and form over time a good, deep red backdrop to both house and garden. I was wrong; it grew quickly and strongly, soon overshadowed roses, day lilies and sundial to the extent that I was left with a tree and sundial. Now, I have a circular planting, half and half, of green and gold forms of creeping Jenny (*Lysimachia nummularia*) and there, matters more or less stand.

I have considered the negative and more positive aspects of my work here and looked at the improver's part with a critical eye. It may seem that I have considered him or her as a phenomenon made instantly whole, instead of composed of various parts not all of which are at peace with each other. In my particular form, the parts are in constant and perhaps unstable flux. When I first topped the hill and looked down into the valley, I immediately assumed the role of the extreme improver – that is the indignant reformer, a kind of crusader. What I saw in front of me was a broken and debased landscape of tumbled down walls and rushy fields and decayed farm buildings. Perhaps, truthfully, this was not quite so much in the eye, as in the mind. In such circumstances, anything done would count as improvement. After that, my role changed fairly rapidly into that of the patriot improver, dedicated to restoring the landscape and restricted to reviving what had been there. This meant a prescriptive enthusiasm for indigenous trees, alders, birch, rowan and Scots pine, and plants such as wild honeysuckle and so on, though I drew the line at the heather family with its rock garden associations. Then along came the improver as a cultivator who put the fields in order and the farm on a commercial footing. That patriot was succeeded, or overshadowed, by the modified aesthete, interested more in expansion rather than contraction, and hearing a different accent in the genius of the place. He understood that the traditional pattern of house and land of this sort was now an anachronism, out of step with both the society and the economics that had sheltered it in the past. And into this vacuum boldly stepped the green knight of forestry. To an improver's eye, the absolute geometry of the forestry monotone needed relief, what tyre mechanics call rebalance, so that new and old might find some sort of harmony in colour and texture, such as any gardener would seek in a border. Unlike the forester who thinks in forty year cycles, or the farmer at the mercy of public funding, the improver, in any form, is in for the long run and knowingly offers all his work as a hostage to fortune.

There is a further aspect to the improver's lot and that is to be too successful. In my case, it was the failure to see things growing out of proportion and to keep the first, fresh sense of scale and balance. The solution, I am afraid, is a somewhat draconian one: it needs the arrival once in a while of a philistine with a sharp eye, a strong sense of the utilitarian and almost complete lack of sympathy. Fortunately, I am married to one. Such harsh advice is always offered uncompromisingly and should be accepted with reluctance, for it usually means regression and an unlooked for and unjustified blow to the aesthetic judgment. Growth, trees and shrubs, have to be objectively judged, for while the tree gets bigger and better and fits the improver's pattern, it simultaneously cuts light, takes space, casts shadows and limits colour. In the garden, after more than twenty years the viburnums are nearly at 15 feet and the dogwood, *Cornus mas*, even higher, all have radically changed the shape and feel of the garden and introduced, I am told, a note of gloom. Beyond the garden, there are similar problems, where the wood has been lost in the trees, and the world of thinning, lopping, brashing, and pruning has been entered. While the improver can take much of this in his stride, the sentimental one has other difficulties, especially in the garden. There, long serving and faithful servants are rewarded with eviction, old beauties are scorned and the daring reproved. Virtue has little reward and the new incomers feted and made much of: there is about it all a plangent air of betrayal.

In parting however, I would like to make clear that work continues and time and money are relentlessly spent. There is, too, the irresistible urge to expand, to try one plant or tree more, sow a wild flower meadow here, plant iris and primula on the burnside there, extend a walk for a few more yards, add another gate, like some Roman imperator viewing the northern frontier from the wall. The only effective break on all of this is maintenance or perhaps the standard of maintenance. As I wrote at the outset, this garden, and the landscape that it forms part, is a one man show. There is really no help on some kind of green alert, or well mechanized nursery round the corner and certainly none that would come near my picky standards. For neatness and tidiness are always necessary to set against the rather casual and slovenly ways of nature; it is part of the natural balance of things. While a certain degree of mess is acceptable from time to time, unpainted gates, over rough grass, unstaked shrubs, hairy hedges, walls without capstones, toppled trees, most can be reluctantly shouldered for a while, so long as there is an end in sight where all will be well. The horror of the opposite, chaos, keeps gardener and the groundsman on their toes and, for that matter, the effective empire within its administrative frontiers. Yet, this suggests more the maintenance man, who washes but does not drive the car, happier in the garage than on the highway and who has never heard the poop-poop of the open road that so mesmerised Toad of Toad Hall as 'the poetry of motion' in *The Wind in the Willows*.

Index